Canals and Railways of Wiltshire

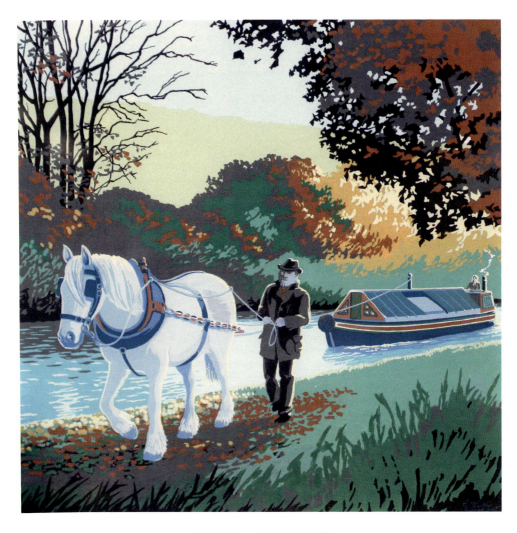

KEN JONES

Title page image: *Horsepower on the Kennet and Avon Canal* by Evelyn Bartlett.

Contents page images:
Left: Class 50 no. 50007 *Hercules* at Fairwood Junction, Westbury, with a Victoria to Exeter St. David's excursion on 18 June 2022.

Right: Class 60 no. 60028 in Cappagh DCRail blue livery with matching wagons heads a Willesden to Machen Quarry empties and is approaching Trowbridge on 5 March 2022.

Acknowledgements
My wife, Elizabeth, for the hours of isolation she has tolerated while I prepared my text and images for publication. There have been times of joint pleasure, however, when we have studied maps together, walked towpaths with our Dachshunds and visited abandoned canal or railway sites. She has also read the narrative, frequently corrected spelling and grammatical mistakes, which are always the fault of the computer!

To artist Evelyn Bartlett for setting the scene in autumn near Burbage. www.evelynbartlett.co.uk

Special thanks to Vivienne Evans for proofreading the text; to Erik Neale, who helped with technical matters; my son Steve for quality photography. Tom Plant of the Wiltshire and Swindon History Centre in Chippenham was helpful; so too was Elaine Arthurs at Steam Museum, Swindon. Salisbury Library helped investigate track diagrams of the Market House Railway and allowed photography of the same. The Signalling Record Society provided information on signal boxes at Swindon. The Kennet and Avon and Wilts and Berks Canal Trusts must not pass unmentioned. In particular, the volunteers at Crofton Pumping Station for their help and enthusiastic cooperation.

Finally, to all the volunteers on canals, narrowboat owners and those in railway preservation that have given me their time and knowledge – a big thank you.

'Come on you two, we've a long way to go.'

A note about the images
The railway photographs included here are almost all from original negatives, colour slides and digital images held in the K&SJ Rail Archive, with many taken by me – the author – and my son. There are a number of Edwardian postcard images, which have been in the public domain for 40 years or more – these are also part of the K&SJ Rail Archive.

All the canal photographs were taken by the author except a small number of early postcards that are in the public domain. Great thanks to all the photographers of the past, whose photographic imaging lives on.

In 1960, I took up railway and general photography, in order to record the contemporary scene. The photographs I took are a historical record of times past. The technology has moved on, but negatives and colour slides, once archived, are still available to be printed even those from more than 100 years ago.

Published by Key Books
An imprint of Key Publishing Ltd
PO Box 100
Stamford
Lincs PE9 1XQ

www.keypublishing.com

The right of Ken Jones to be identified as the author of this book has been asserted in accordance with the Copyright, Designs and Patents Act 1988 Sections 77 and 78.

Copyright © Ken Jones, 2024

ISBN 978 1 80282 955 6

Typeset by SJmagic DESIGN SERVICES, India.

Contents

Introduction

I have had a lifelong interest in railways and canals, stemming from my childhood in Buckinghamshire to where my family moved from the Rhondda Valley in the 1930s. We lived in a flat near Uxbridge. It was on the road to Wales but also only a mile to the Grand Union Canal of which I have fond memories. In the 1940s, our holidays were taken at the family home in Wales, or to my grandmother on my mother's side, in a little village near Orpington, Kent. Both journeys involved trains.

At the age of ten, we moved to the village of Iver, near the Slough arm of the Grand Union Canal and the former Great Western Main Line. In later years, from here, I took regular excursions into Wiltshire to visit the railway works at Swindon. As I travelled down the main line after Didcot, I discovered that this was the route of the Wilts and Berks Canal on its way to Abingdon, closed and abandoned for half a century.

After a move to Reading, I discovered the remains of the Kennet and Avon Canal and the joy of having a railway line, the Berks and Hants, running parallel with it almost all the way from Theale to Savernake. This was a happy hunting ground for photographs, combining water and rail and I am pleased to have recorded the scene of dereliction on the canal prior to its full restoration.

Today, seemingly impossible restoration projects are alive and prospering, but what a daunting task they face. I now experience the restoration of Wiltshire canals first hand as I live in the county, and with my wife and dogs have enjoyed walking the towpath of the Kennet and

The 12.30 Paddington to Paignton runs alongside the Kennet and Avon Canal at Froxfield with Class 47 no. 47488 in charge on 29 August 1978.

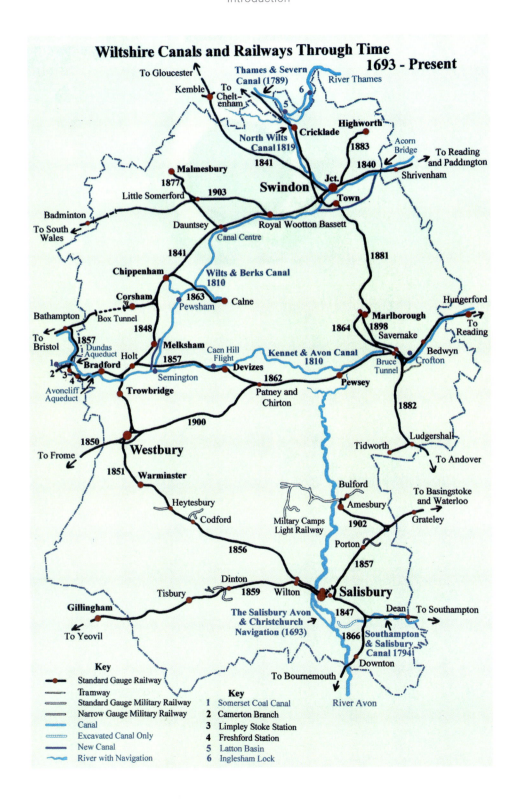

Wiltshire Canals and Railways Through Time
1693 - Present

To Gloucester
Kemble
To Chelt-enham
Thames & Severn Canal (1789)
River Thames
6
5
North Wilts Canal 1819
1841
Cricklade
Highworth
1883
Acorn Bridge
1840
To Reading and Paddington
Shrivenham
Malmesbury
1877
Little Somerford
1903
Jct.
Swindon
Town
Dauntsey
Royal Wootton Bassett
Canal Centre
Badminton
To South Wales
1841
1881
Chippenham
Wilts & Berks Canal 1810
Corsham
1863
Pewsham
Calne
Hungerford
Bathampton
Box Tunnel
1848
Marlborough
1864
1898
Savernake
To Reading
To Bristol
1857
Dundas Aqueduct
Holt
Melksham
1857
Caen Hill Flight
Kennet & Avon Canal 1810
Bedwyn
Crofton
Bruce Tunnel
1
2
3
4
Bradford
Semington
Devizes
1862
Patney and Chirton
Pewsey
Avoncliff Aqueduct
Trowbridge
1882
1900
Ludgershall
1850
Westbury
Tidworth
To Andover
To Frome
1851
Warminster
Bulford
Amesbury
To Basingstoke and Waterloo
Grateley
Heytesbury
Codford
Miltary Camps Light Railway
1902
Porton
1857
1856
Dinton
Tisbury
1859
Wilton
Salisbury
Dean
To Southampton
Gillingham
The Salisbury Avon & Christchurch Navigation (1693)
1847
1866
Southampton & Salisbury Canal 1794
To Yeovil
Downton
To Bournemouth
River Avon

Key
- Standard Gauge Railway
- Tramway
- Standard Gauge Military Railway
- Narrow Gauge Military Railway
- Canal
- Excavated Canal Only
- New Canal
- River with Navigation

Key
1 Somerset Coal Canal
2 Camerton Branch
3 Limpley Stoke Station
4 Freshford Station
5 Latton Basin
6 Inglesham Lock

Broad-gauge locomotive *Iron Duke* rests on a flatrol wagon at Westbury yard open day on 5 May 1985. *Iron Duke* was built as a replica, in 1984, following drawings provided by Resco (Railway Works). Note its wooden boiler cladding, which dates the locomotive to pre-1848, when the wooden lagging on locomotives was covered in sheet iron.

Avon Canal. The Swindon and Cricklade Railway, a heritage site, is also a pleasure, as are the railway centres of Salisbury, Swindon and Westbury.

The canals and railways of Britain are inexorably linked and receive equal prominence in this title. In east Wiltshire where the Kennet and Avon Canal leaves Berkshire at Froxfield following its westward course, the Berks and Hants extension line of the old Great Western Railway runs in close association with the canal as far as Savernake, where the K&A's Bruce Tunnel is located. Happily, this provides the means of including rail and water in the same photographic composition.

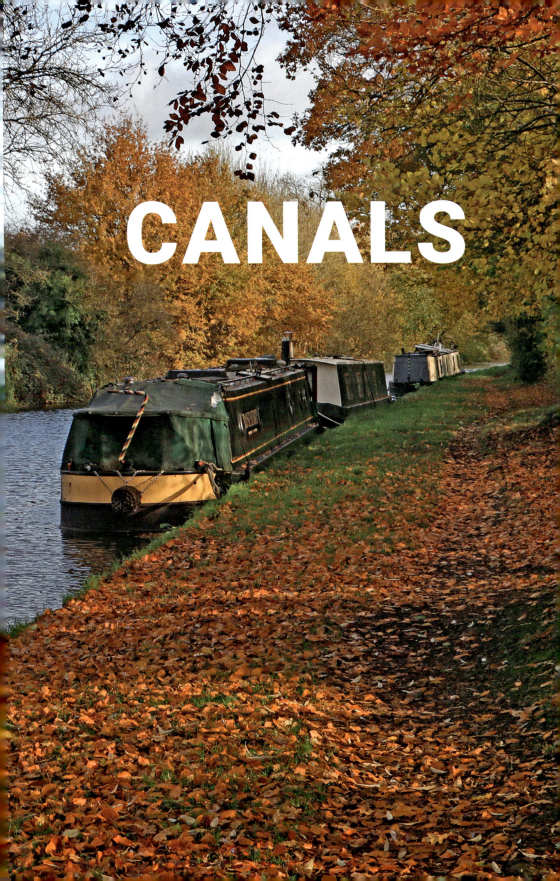

CANALS

Chapter 1

Canal Lore

Building Britain's canals

Navigable waterways in Britain have been used as a means of transporting goods since pre-Roman times. However, the Industrial Revolution (*c1760*) created a need for more efficient movement of raw materials and finished products and that caused a spurt of artificial waterway construction. Construction began in the Potteries; canals were smooth and gentle, resulting in the transportation of finished products without the breakages caused by bumping precious cargoes along uneven roads.

Road systems and surfaces were poor up to the middle of the 18th century and inadequate for the transportation of heavy loads on a continual basis. A train of pack horses and a heavily laden cart were the only means of bulk carrying of goods. The wheels of horse-drawn carts and wagons, particularly in winter, would rut the road. In the worst winters, goods transportation became impossible.

Canals were never designed for carrying passengers; journey times were long and could take days to complete, particularly if there were many locks to negotiate. Nevertheless, packet boats did carry passengers, mail and parcels. The time taken to deliver raw materials and finished

A scene that could be from the 1920s were it not for the houseboat with a cycle on the roof. This scene, shot in 2003, near Staverton, on the Kennet and Avon Canal, shows a powered cargo narrowboat, *Almighty*, towing an unpowered butty, *Kestrel*. The butty, or companion boat, had no engine and was used in tow to increase the payload. The carrying of freight long distances by canals generally ceased by 1970.

goods was comparable with movement by road, as both systems involved the use of horses as motive power. Significantly, a horse-drawn barge (*see* Narrowboats) could carry ten times the payload of a horse-drawn wagon for the same horsepower requirement and there were no steep hills involving the risk of the load being too heavy for the horses to manage the incline.

There were two concentrated periods of canal building, between *c*1760 and *c*1775 and from 1789 until 1800, by which time the country was latticed with navigable waterways and canals. Some were narrow, with locks capable of lifting one barge at a time, while others were built as wide canals with locks holding barges side by side. In the heyday of canal construction there were many abortive schemes, some of which were started and later abandoned through geological or financial reasons.

Early canals followed the contours of the land in an attempt to maintain a level course and to avoid the necessity of digging out tunnels, building aqueducts or creating high-rise flights of locks – this was indeed the long way round. Later canals continued to follow the gentler contours of the land but disregarded major obstructions and took a straighter course involving major civil engineering in the construction. Many canals followed river valleys and made use of the rivers wherever possible to minimise canal construction costs. Inevitably, a river valley rises (with sea level as a datum) as it nears the river's source, thus the passage of the canal in the river valley also needs to rise. The change in water level is achieved with the help of a lock, and the lie of the land determines the frequency of lock requirement.

Locks

Canals had to be made watertight, after which there was a constant need to ensure that the level of water was maintained, particularly with the necessity of locks to cater for rising and falling gradients. Locks have a fixed chamber with gates at both ends – these are called pound locks, because the locks are situated between pounds (lengths) of water. In wide canals, the lock has a

Closing the lock gates at Seend Cleeve on the Kennet and Avon Canal. Here the canal rises to the Devizes Caen Hill flight only a few miles away, but the summit of the canal is further on, at Crofton, where the canal is fed by a pumping station and a reservoir.

A scene near Whaddon on a level stretch of canal between Semington and Bradford on Avon.

chamber wide enough for two barges to sit side by side, but, of course, both must be travelling in the same direction. A barge enters the lock and the gates are closed behind it to secure the barge safely within. To raise the water level and barge to the new level of the canal, a rack and pinion system (winding gear) is operated manually to raise a paddle or sluice that allows water from the higher canal to enter the chamber and eventually raise the barge to the higher level. It is usual for each bargee to have their own windlass or winding key to operate the winding gear. It is vital to ensure the paddle in the lower gates is closed to prevent water draining from the chamber as it is being filled. When level water is reached (the water is equalised) the gates can be opened and the barge can leave the chamber. Each time a lock gate is opened, water is lost from the summit and there is a need to replenish with a natural or engineered water source.

For a barge needing to access a lower level of the canal (downstream), it enters the chamber and the upper gates are closed behind it, ensuring the paddle or sluice is also closed at the upper level. Once the barge (narrowboat) is secured in the chamber the lower paddle (sluice gate) can be opened allowing water to drain from the chamber into the lower level of the canal. When level water is reached the lower gates can be opened and the barge can continue its journey.

Wide canals have two gates at each end called half gates. Two half gates, when closed, create a 'pointing gate'. Each half gate closes to an 18-degree point (144-degree internal gate angle) creating a chevron. The point faces upstream so that the water pressure keeps the gates closed. Each half gate has a balance arm pointing landward, which balances the gate and allows leverage to open and close the gate with a minimum of manual effort. The lower gates are always deeper than the upper gates, the extra depth equivalent to the lock's water level rise. When gates and paddles are closed, they should be watertight, but in practice there are frequent water spouts emanating from poor joins or aged and ill-fitting gates.

Narrow canals have a chamber that takes only one narrowboat and there is only one lock gate at each end.

For deep, abrupt changes in water level, pound locks are unsuitable. The fixed chamber becomes a moving watertight chamber in a boat lift. The chamber in this system is called a 'caisson' and rises and falls to reach an upper or lower level respectively. This system does not operate on Wiltshire's canals.

Narrowboats

To use the term 'barge' in reference to canal boats is technically incorrect – 'narrowboat' is the accurate terminology. They are flat-bottom craft originally built in the 18th and 19th centuries as working boats for the narrow canals of Britain. Barges are much wider cargo vessels for ship canals and wide, navigable rivers. A narrowboat is generally less than 7ft wide to ensure it can navigate and pass other craft on narrow canal systems. The boat must generally have a maximum length of 70ft to ensure it can enter and be contained in locks without being upended on the concrete sill of the upper gate when the chamber is emptied.

Many modern narrowboats are built for hire or used as house boats. They are generally shorter than the old freighters. The boats are skilfully made to have the same manufactured appearance as the living cabins of old working boats, but modern materials and manufacturing methods are used to lessen the cost and provide contemporary convenience.

The first narrowboats for cargo were horse-drawn by rope. There were no living quarters; the bargee, or boatman, had to find accommodation at the end of his working day. It was a natural progression to include a boatman's cabin on the narrowboat, but of course this reduced the payload. Once steam power and later diesel engines were introduced, replacing horses as motive power, it became feasible for a companion or butty boat to be towed. This dramatically increased the carrying capacity and allowed a bigger family cabin in the principal boat.

Railway competition

The construction of the railways from the origination of the Stockton and Darlington in 1825, in an ever-expanding network, ultimately brought about the demise of canals, the mode of transporting goods that had developed in the latter half of the preceding century. This shift from the waterways to the railways was gradual, as more villages, towns and cities became accessible by a faster and more efficient railway network. From 1840, when railways slowly began to replace canals as the most efficient mode of transport, the days of the packet boat had ended, but canals were still used to transport minerals, timber and goods for some years to come, despite the greater capacity of long goods trains. Over time, canal cargo volumes decreased.

Beyond the middle of the 19th century, railways became dominant since they were cheaper to construct than digging cuts in the landscape. Often, rail companies took over the assets of the canal companies to eliminate what little competition there was, then failed to invest in their maintenance. Surprisingly, long-distance freight did not finally cease on Britain's canals until 1970, assisted by the big freeze of 1963, when many canals were frozen for up to three months, and what little trade remained transferred to rail and road.

The dwindling use of canals into the 20th century caused locks to decay and water channels to silt up. Once a lock gate rots and releases water, the canal starts to drain. With no financial incentive for canals to continue, those that had fallen out of use quickly became intermittent lengths of lake. Only the main thoroughfare canals such as the Grand Union remained navigable.

Later came the realisation that the country's canal heritage was being lost and preservation groups and societies were launched with ambitions to restore Britain's canals. The Kennet and Avon in Wiltshire is a case in point – the complete canal length, including the enormous task of restoring the Devizes Caen Hill flight of locks, is open for all who choose to boat, walk or cycle along its tow path.

Chapter 2

Wiltshire's Canals

The principal canal waterway through Wiltshire is the Kennet and Avon. Joining it at Semington was the Wilts and Berks Canal, which is currently being restored and once took a broadly north-easterly course via Swindon to join the River Thames at Abingdon. The North Wilts branch of the Wilts and Berks Canal joined the Thames and Severn Canal at Latton, in north Wiltshire, and when restored will inevitably be constructed through built-up areas, as there is very little of the original left in situ. There are a number of branches from the Wilts and Berks Canal to important towns throughout the route – the Wiltshire extensions were to Calne and Chippenham.

The existence of a canal between Southampton and Salisbury is not well known. Indeed, it was never completed, but dry excavated sections remain in Alderbury and East Grimstead towards West Dean. Original proposals considered joining this canal route to the Kennet and Avon at Pewsey. A second man-made navigation channel still exists in Salisbury, south through the village of Britford, although the Salisbury Avon and Christchurch Navigation, as it was known, can no longer be navigated. Another possibility was a connection to Pewsey via the Avon Navigation.

Right: The remains of the Calne branch of the Wilts & Berks Canal at Calne, showing Chavey Well Bridge (ST 998 705).

Below: A narrowboat turns to face the opposite direction in a 'winding hole'. Each winding hole has a maximum turning circle marked on a post – usually up to 72ft.

Chapter 3

The Southampton and Salisbury Canal

The map of the Southampton and Salisbury Canal (not to scale). Roads are included if they are relevant so the reader may discover the remains of the canal.

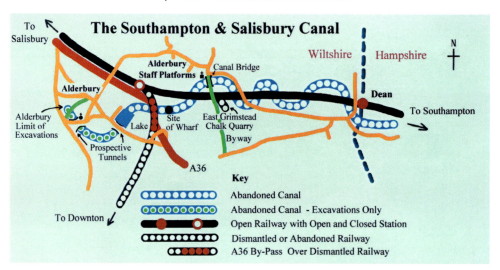

All that remains of the Southampton to Salisbury canal are earthworks. Its purpose was so short lived, in fact, that it never reached Salisbury. Its navigable limit was Alderbury/Whaddon Common, near Salisbury. Earthworks of the unfinished canal are still evident skirting the high ground around the centre of Alderbury towards the village of Shute End, on its proposed route into Salisbury. Most of the remaining visible evidence of the canal is in Wiltshire.

An Act of Parliament permitting construction of a canal between Redbridge (at the head of Southampton Water) and Redbridge was passed in 1789; that canal opened in 1794.

A new canal between Redbridge and Salisbury had been mooted in 1768 after engineer James Brindley had surveyed a possible route. Another canal course, Redbridge to Andover, was surveyed two years later, and it was agreed that it made sense to join the canals as one waterway en route to reach Redbridge. The proposals foundered in 1772.

The Salisbury arm of the canal was surveyed again in 1793, this time by Joseph Hill, when the Andover canal was well under way to completion. Hill estimated the cost to be £50,000, which included a section through Southampton, mostly in a tunnel, designed to connect with God's House Tower, a building in the south-east corner of the town walls, and the harbour, with a short branch to connect with the river Itchen. The Act of Parliament for construction of the Southampton to Salisbury canal was passed in 1795.

Initially, the idea of a canal that would eventually reach Bristol received local support and a great deal of Bristolian interest, but the project was short of shareholders from the outset. Contracts were signed on 15 October 1795, with Joseph Hill as engineer and, by the end of 1796, arrangements were agreed to reach Alderbury Common (about 60 miles from Bristol). An instalment of the £100 share issues was called in from the shareholders to enable work to commence.

The Southampton extension from Redbridge of the Southampton to Salisbury Canal was contracted to Thomas Jinkins, but a report into the work suggested that the materials and workmanship were inadequate. Jinkins was requested to make good the defects prior to any cash payments for the work he had completed. With cash withheld, he was unable to pay the workers or buy materials, resulting in writs being served upon him.

Excluding the Andover canal section between Redbridge and Kimbridge, there were 14 locks planned as far as Alderbury Common and another two on the Southampton extension, one for access to the Itchen and another to Southampton Water/River Test estuary at God's House Tower. On the section planned but never built out of Alderbury to Salisbury, a minimum of three locks was necessary. The maximum length of boat accepted into the locks was 60ft and the maximum boat beam was 8ft. This suggests that all the locks were narrow, possibly with a single gate at each end to keep costs to a minimum. The width of the canal was 15ft across the base, widening to 27ft at the surface with a flat depth of 4ft in the centre. Two reservoirs were necessary at Alderbury and West Grimstead to feed the canal.

In 1798, Rennie was asked to inspect the whole ongoing canal works. He reported that progress had been made, but too little and too late. By the time John Rennie became chief engineer in 1799, funds had dried up and all the shareholders' money had been spent. Bad weather in 1799 caused serious flooding to the canal, sweeping away West Dean Bridge and causing lock damage.

A new Act of Parliament was required to authorise the raising of more funds to complete the canal. This occurred in 1800, allowing an additional £10,000 to the original £30,000 to be raised by mortgage. Money was slow forthcoming, but sufficient to allow work to recommence on the Kimbridge to Salisbury arm. In 1801, George Jones was appointed as engineer on the recommendation of Rennie to assist him by taking the brunt of the work. By 1802, the canal was navigable and in use as far as West Dean. The canal ran parallel upstream with the river Dun into Wiltshire and left the village centre under a two-arched bridge, one for the canal and one for the river, with the canal arch on the left of the river viewing upstream.

The canal followed the contours of the land to reach East then West Grimstead. The canal bed is traceable on the Ordnance Survey through to West Grimstead, but is less obvious once it passes under the only canal bridge surviving on the route after the Southampton to Salisbury railway line was built on some of the canal formation.

By 1803, the canal had reached Alderbury/Whaddon Common and was in use as far as the wharf. A deep cutting was necessary from here to the old Southampton to Salisbury turnpike (the old A36), which took a course through Whaddon and Alderbury villages. The canal was meant to enter a tunnel here about 100 yards long to avoid interrupting the route of the turnpike. To build a wharf any nearer the turnpike would have been unsuitable due to the lie of the land and the need to tunnel under the turnpike. As a temporary measure, it was decided to construct a wooden horse railway, which George Jones assessed could be

The idyllic village green and river in the centre of West Dean. The canal ran parallel with the river at this location on its left side. The present bridge, seen in the photograph, dates from the 1930s and replaced a two-arched bridge. (SU 257 269)

It is difficult to believe that there was a lock in the foreground of this location. The only evidence is the last vestige of brickwork. (SU 246 271)

Right: Inevitably, a disused linear feature in the landscape becomes difficult to trace due to undergrowth and, in the case of old canals, infilled with leaf mould and side wall slippage, decreasing the depth significantly. This view of the bed of the old Southampton to Salisbury Canal is remarkably well preserved as it heads for East Grimstead from West Dean. (SU 246 271)

Below: The sole surviving bridge on the canal, which carries a byway near East Grimstead church. (SU 225 273)

Above left: After the site of Alderbury Wharf, the canal excavation swings south-west, parallel now with Firs Road. Here the cut deepens with stagnant water, which appears to be stained with iron oxide.

Above right: On the approach to the old Salisbury to Southampton turnpike, the canal bed enters a rectangular lake. The turnpike is known locally as the 'old A36', through the villages of Alderbury and Whaddon. The current A36 bypasses the villages severing the route of the canal (both SU 194 270).

Below: The end of the water-filled canal in Alderbury adjacent to present-day Firs Road, as seen in 1910. Now a lake, the body of water has the appearance of an old canal basin. Spoil from the building of the bypass was dumped in the vicinity, affecting drainage and resulting in the lake seen today.

built for less than £65. A wooden horse railway was a narrow-gauge track with wooden sleepers and probably wooden rails. This early type of tramway carrying wagons was pulled by horses. The freight or minerals were loaded on to wagons and taken to the turnpike for onward transit into Salisbury.

Once the canal was open for traffic between the west end of the Southampton tunnel and Alderbury Common wharf, there were incentives to encourage trade. In 1802, the tolls were set at 2d per ton per mile, but soon after lowered. Chalk, lime and other horticultural manures were reduced to half toll at 1d per mile and all other goods reduced to 1½d per ton per mile. The canal was used, but not enough to pay its way.

The destination of Salisbury had not been achieved. With no money to continue, despite excavations through Alderbury to the other side of Silver Street and little more than two miles to go to achieve its Milford destination, further requests for finance met with deaf ears. Traffic declined, and by 1806 the condition of the canal had deteriorated such that in 1808 it was closed.

The intended tunnel under the old A36 was never completed. The excavated route remembered by Canal Lane on the west side of the old A36 follows the contours turning north-west through private land below Alderbury House to a short, intended tunnel under the minor road below Alderbury Church, remembering the route of the canal in its name, Tunnel Hill.

Here is a well preserved, dry, excavated stretch of the intended canal, which crosses a field with public rights of way. Although the rights of way follow a straight course across the field, the obvious path takes a meandering route closer to the canal, allowing observation.

Three reminders of the existence of a canal in Alderbury, although all commemorate the excavation, which never saw any traffic and most of it no water either.

The excavated dry canal south of Alderbury church. The trough shape can clearly be seen, despite natural infill since 1808. The view is towards Silver Street and the proposed route into Salisbury. (SU 181 269)

Chapter 4

Salisbury, Avon and Christchurch Navigation

lthough there had been soundings about navigation from Salisbury to the sea in the
16th century, the first positive action to join the two took place in 1664, a century
before canal construction got underway. An Act of Parliament authorised the Earl
of Clarendon to make the 36 miles from Salisbury to Christchurch navigable along the river
Avon. The Avon is the river rising in two tributaries north and west of Pewsey and joining
forces at Upavon. It is known locally as the Salisbury or Hampshire Avon, distinct from the
Avon that flows through Bradford on Avon, which is joined by the Kennet and Avon Canal at
Bath. Unfortunately, the only work carried out was at Christchurch Quay.

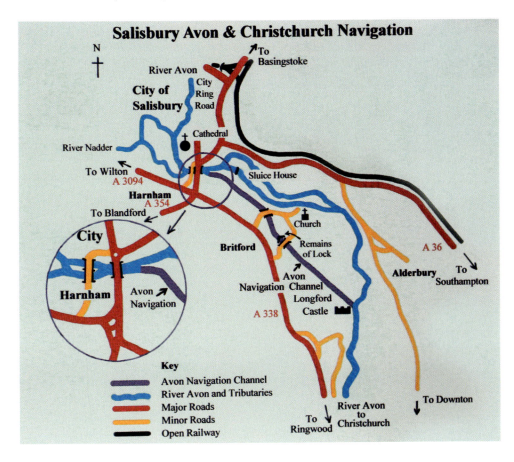

In 1675, Lord Salisbury asked Andrew Yarrenton to survey the river for feasibility of achieving the river navigation and it was concluded that a navigation channel was feasible. The cause was taken up by Salisbury Corporation because it could see distinct benefits for a direct waterway to the south coast. Work began in September 1675, with Samuel Fortrey as engineer with a fund of £2,000. However, the council could not get sufficient support and discontinued the work in 1677.

Subsequently private individuals continued financing the work and the river became navigable by 1684, when two 25-ton barges reached the city. In 1687, a Code of Regulations and a system of tolls was issued.

The main navigation cuts were constructed in 1693 and after, when another group financed improvements to eliminate difficult navigation on the main stream of the river. In 1699, a bill was placed before parliament for increased powers, but it failed and interest in the Avon navigation waned.

Another group interested in achieving a prosperous river Avon navigation took over improvements in 1702. It built bridges over the navigation and probably the three locks in the navigation channels, but its efforts were short-lived and navigation ceased in 1705. Further attempts were made in 1730 by Salisbury Corporation but this too failed and there were no further navigation efforts.

Above: The River Avon from the modern Harnham Bridge. Here the river forks downstream, the left arm is the main river stream and on the right is the navigation channel, which is blocked for craft (out of view). (SU 145 291)

Left: The Avon navigation channel at Britford looking downstream towards Longford Castle. (SU 159 278)

It is unlikely that there were any horse-towing paths, so any barge attempting to reach Salisbury must have done so with sail. The boundary between Wiltshire and Hampshire passes across the river a little south of Downton.

Beyond the Salisbury navigation channel, between the Harnham Bridge and Longford Castle, where one lock existed, there were cut channels at Downton, Horsport (near Fordingbridge) with a lock, Ellingham, Ringwood, Avon, Sopley and then Winkton with the last lock. Since the 18th century, many drainage channels have been cut for the water meadows and tracing the navigation channels is difficult south of Longford Castle.

Right: The remains of Britford lock on the navigation channel between Salisbury and Longford Castle. This view is upstream towards Harnham, Salisbury. The sluice gate at the head of the old lock dates from the 19th century. (SU 159 278)

Below: The mainstream of the river Avon as it approaches Downton. Here the Avon Valley Walk between Salisbury and Christchurch touches upon the river on its meandering route through woodland and meadow. (SU 176 220)

Chapter 5

The Kennet and Avon Canal

The Kennet and Avon Canal is just short of 87 miles long, consisting of 57 miles of canal, in its purest sense, joining the River Kennet navigation between Newbury and Reading to the east, where it joins the Thames. In the west, the canal meets the River Avon at Bath, which is navigable to Bristol and eventually to Avonmouth.

The River Kennet was made navigable between Newbury and the Thames at Reading in 1723, by creating locks and artificial cuts or pounds to cater for the natural fall of the river. Where a lock lowers the navigation on a river, the river itself passes over a weir to the side of the lock, subsequently achieving the same water level at each side of the lock. At Bath, the canal joins the River Avon navigation, completed in 1727, as far as Hanham lock.

Having engineered navigable water between Bristol and Bath and Newbury and the Thames it was inevitable that an artificial canal should be promoted to create a through navigable waterway between the Bristol Channel and London. The canal was constructed after the passing of various acts of Parliament between 1794 and the opening of the canal on 28 December 1810. The Caen Hill flight of locks in Devizes was the last section to be completed.

The canal prospered between its opening and *c*1850, when the effect of railway construction began to sap trade from the much slower waterway. The construction of railways between Reading and Bath along the Kennet valley was piecemeal; there was not a through route to Bristol via Westbury until 1900 on the Berks and Hants railway line. The principal railway route created by the Great Western Railway (GWR) connecting London with Bristol was via Swindon and opened in 1840.

The Kennet and Avon Canal and the GWR were in direct competition with each other. Inevitably, the canal trade declined through inability to compete, resulting in the Kennet and

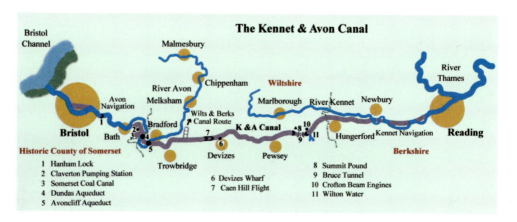

The Kennet & Avon Canal

Bristol Channel
Malmesbury
River Thames
River Avon
Chippenham
Wiltshire
Avon Navigation
Melksham
Marlborough River Kennet Newbury
Bristol
Bath
Bradford
Wilts & Berks Canal Route
K & A Canal
Hungerford
Kennet Navigation
Reading

Historic County of Somerset
1 Hanham Lock
2 Claverton Pumping Station
3 Somerset Coal Canal
4 Dundas Aqueduct
5 Avoncliff Aqueduct

Trowbridge
Devizes
Pewsey

6 Devizes Wharf
7 Caen Hill Flight

8 Summit Pound
9 Bruce Tunnel
10 Crofton Beam Engines
11 Wilton Water

Berkshire

Avon Canal offering its operation and assets to the GWR, which accepted, taking control in 1852. Clearly it was in the interests of the GWR to promote its railway operation in preference to the less efficient canal. However, there was still canal wharf to wharf traffic, which was convenient for local movement of goods.

After 1877, the Kennet and Avon Canal never realised a profit. Investment in its infrastructure reduced as its income waned. Further decline in the condition of the waterway was seen when lock gates began to deteriorate. Even the successful Somerset Coal Canal, which joined the Kennet and Avon adjacent to Dundas Aqueduct, near Limpley Stoke, started to lose trade after railway colliery connections were made in the mid-1870s. The coal canal was declared derelict in 1903.

The Wilts & Berks Canal, which joined the Kennet and Avon at Semington, suffered severe decline in business towards the end of the 19th century. Traffic to and from the Kennet and Avon practically ceased after the collapse of Stanley Aqueduct in 1901, compounded in 1906 when the canal burst its banks, which led to the abandonment of the canal in 1914.

Although the Kennet and Avon canal was still navigable by 1930, there was very little traffic and hardly any encouragement from the GWR. In 1948, the big four railway companies were nationalised and the Kennet and Avon, through ownership by the GWR, was taken over by the Railway Executive. Attempts were made to make good the poor level of maintenance over the preceding decades. This involved dredging silted-up pounds and lock chambers. This was to little avail as leaky, unmaintained lock gates caused low water levels in several pounds and consequent disruption to traffic.

In 1949, control of the canal was transferred to the Docks and Inland Waterways Executive. A year later, a stoppage was declared at Heales Lock, near Woolhampton in Berkshire, due to the precarious condition of the lock gates, which were padlocked to prevent opening. Although repaired, the overall condition of the remainder of the canal, particularly on the Caen Hill flight, deteriorated to a level that became impassable by 1952. Isolated sections of the canal were still navigable, predominantly for pleasure craft.

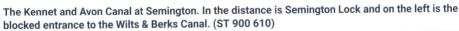

The Kennet and Avon Canal at Semington. In the distance is Semington Lock and on the left is the blocked entrance to the Wilts & Berks Canal. (ST 900 610)

The entrance to the Somerset Coal Canal near Dundas Aqueduct. The entrance to the canal is just over the Wiltshire county boundary in Somerset. (ST 784 626)

A drained pound of the Kennet and Avon at Seend in February 2012. The canal appears quite shallow, despite tapering to the centre. No doubt there was a thick layer of mud to remove before refilling. (ST 930 614)

The Inland Waterways Association was formed in 1946 and soon after, a subdivision of this body called the Kennet and Avon Canal Association was inaugurated. This association of members interested in promoting and preserving the Kennet and Avon Canal subsequently made plans to restore and reopen the waterway. There were many obstacles to overcome, not helped by changes in the controlling authority. In 1962, the association was reformed into the Kennet and Avon Canal Trust Ltd, a non-profit-making organisation, to facilitate the restoration.

On New Year's Day 1963, a new administration commenced, known as the British Waterways Board. With enthusiastic determination, cooperation from the authorities, much fundraising and many grants from the councils through which the canal passed, work began on lock repairs and ensuring that the canal bed was watertight. The most daunting task on the whole canal was the Caen Hill flight, which by then was derelict.

On 8 August 1990, the full length of the canal opened for the second time, almost 180 years after its first inauguration. However, this time, instead of carrying goods, its main purpose was recreation, with many houseboats lining the banks.

The dereliction of Crofton Lock, seen on 8 July 1980. The lock gates were rotten and required replacement. Class 50 no. 50006 *Neptune* hurries past with the 09.15 Penzance to Paddington.

Right: Lock 58 at Crofton, derelict in May 1981.

Below: Caen Hill flight of locks, derelict in May 1981. The canal appears as a stream, but some brickwork had been replaced on the lower lock walls at this point, starting the daunting task of restoring the whole flight.

Chapter 6

Walking the Kennet and Avon Canal

T his book describes the section of the Kennet and Avon Canal that is in Wiltshire. Wiltshire's boundary with Berkshire is Froxfield Bridge and this makes a convenient start point.

The towpath through the county is 40 miles long with 57 locks. The most significant features on the route are Crofton Pumping Station, Bruce Tunnel, Caen Hill flight of locks at Devizes and the aqueducts at Avoncliff and Dundas, near Limpley Stoke. The Berks and Hants railway line runs parallel with the canal almost all the way from Froxfield to Bruce Tunnel at Savernake. To see the canal at its best, narrowboats need to be using the waterway, often an essential ingredient in a successfully composed photograph. The canal is still well used by craft up to the middle of November.

Each of the following maps show walks and points of interest along the canal in sequence from east to west and are mostly five or six miles in length on a destination and return basis. Walking the same stretch of towpath forward and reverse is equally rewarding, as the features are seen in a different perspective. Access to the towpath or parking arrangements may necessitate taking some walking stages in the opposite direction, but the sense of walking the canal there and back will be the same.

At Froxfield Bridge, the start point of my walk on the boundary with Berkshire, there is a winding hole (as in meteorological wind). The length of boats that can be

Rope burns in the masonry on Fore Bridge from the days of horse-drawn haulage of barges and narrowboats. (SU 296 665)

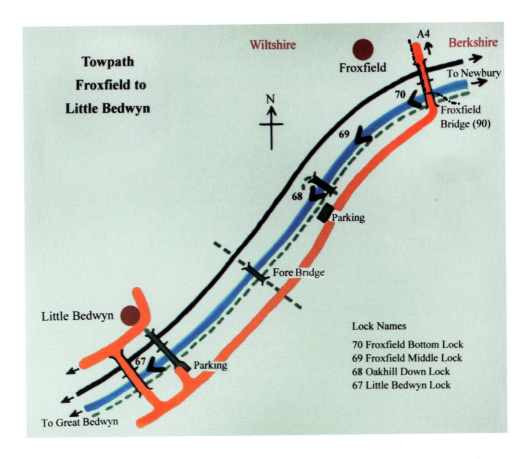

turned is generally between 65ft and 72ft. Within a short distance of the bridge is Froxfield Bottom Lock (70), a favourite location of mine in the 1970s for combining the railway and canal in a single photograph. A short distance further is Froxfield Middle Lock (69), followed by Oakhill Down Lock (68).

From Oakhill Down Lock, the towpath strikes a south-westerly direction and Fore Bridge is soon reached. There is clear evidence of the days of horse-drawn narrowboats on the masonry of the bridge – a series of rope burns dig deep into the stone portal of the bridge. The canal narrows as it goes under the bridge. As the horse reached the wider canal on the other side, the rope scuffed the masonry as it tightens with horsepower.

There is a convenient seat for 'gongoozlers' to watch the canal traffic at Little Bedwyn Lock, the end of this stage of the walk. For the uninitiated, in canal terminology a gongoozler is a person watching canal activities, particularly at locks, without participating in the narrowboat experience.

Continuing from Little Bedwyn towards Great Bedwyn, as Great Bedwyn Wharf Bridge is reached, the railway station is on the right. It is worthwhile walking over the canal and railway bridges to venture down Church Street (on the left) to the Post Office, which has a number of stone grave slabs with amusing epitaphs fixed to its frontage. Returning to the canal, immediately beyond the bridge is the wharf.

The bridges and locks are numbered on the Kennet and Avon Canal. This is Froxfield Bridge no. 90 on the county boundary. (SU 306 678)

Class 50 no. 50012 *Benbow* with a freight passes Froxfield Bottom Lock (70) on 29 August 1978. Note the lock gates had recently been restored. Immediately behind the locomotive is a brake tender, used when the brakes on the locomotive were considered inadequate to control an unfitted goods train. (SU 304 677)

The view east from bridge 91, Oakhill Down, which is adjacent to the lock of the same name. A storm had just passed to leave this idyllic scene on 9 October 2014. (SU 299 672)

50002 *Superb* races past the derelict Little Bedwyn Lock (67) with a West of England to Paddington express on 2 August 1977. At the far end of the lock, the water had been dammed to keep the pound full above the lock. (SU 291 660)

Little Bedwyn Lock again, but now restored and in full use. At the head of the train is HST power car 43033 with a Paddington to Penzance service on 28 September 2016. (SU 291 660) There are two locks on the way to Great Bedwyn, Potters Lock (66) and Burnt Mill (65). A considerable amount of undergrowth had grown on the trackside between my photographic sessions in the 1970s and the present day. Attempting to replicate scenes of 'then and now' were impossible.

A narrowboat emerges from Burnt Mill Lock (65) in October 2016. The canal was well used on that day, evident by the murky water stirred up by many craft. (SU 285 649)

Great Bedwyn Wharf in October 2016, with the first signs of autumn. (SU 280 644)

The canal at Great Bedwyn on 2 February 1977. It has a blanket of floating frogbit weed below which is clear water. The railway runs in front of Great Bedwyn church and was host to an empty stone train hauled by Class 47 no. 47060 bound for a Somerset quarry. (SU 277 642)

The canal seen from Beech Tree Walk Bridge overlooking Beech Grove Lock (63) in October 2016. Further along the canal is a disused bridge covered in concrete tank traps, a remnant of World War Two. The next stage restarts at Little Bedwyn and takes the towpath to Crofton Bridge. (SU 272 632)

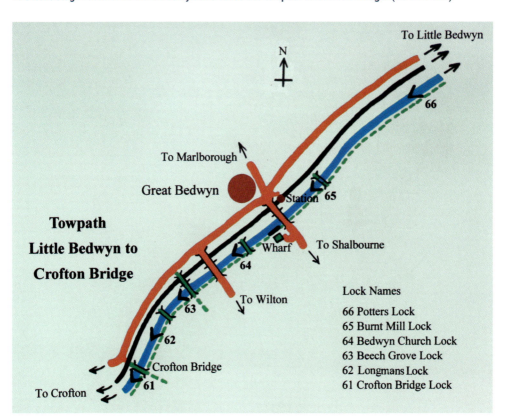

To Little Bedwyn

N

To Marlborough

Great Bedwyn

Station   65

66

Towpath
Little Bedwyn to
Crofton Bridge

Wharf   To Shalbourne

64

To Wilton

63

Lock Names

66 Potters Lock
65 Burnt Mill Lock
64 Bedwyn Church Lock
63 Beech Grove Lock
62 Longmans Lock
61 Crofton Bridge Lock

62

Crofton Bridge

61

To Crofton

This was one of 19 owned by the Kennet and Avon Canal Company, which opened in stages as the civil engineering was completed between main centres. The section between Hungerford and Great Bedwyn was opened on 2 July 1799 to much celebration. The wharf handled incoming traffic of coal, timber, and Bath stone and outgoing barges took grain, wool and a coarse, low-grade cloth.

There is a winding hole after Great Bedwyn Wharf, followed by a view of the church to the right and a lock and bridge aptly named Bedwyn Church Lock (64) and Bedwyn Church Bridge. Further on, Mill Bridge is reached. The canal continues in a south-westerly direction to reach Beech Tree Walk Bridge.

There is evidence here of defences set up in the event of a German invasion expected after the bombing blitz of British towns and cities in World War Two. The Kennet and Avon Canal was used as a barrier, or stop line, and called the General Headquarters Blue Line, which after Semington joined the Green Line to form a water barrier from the Thames to the Avon. On the bridges, there were tank traps, with key bridges and open stretches of waterway covered by pill boxes, either adjacent to a bridge on the north bank of the canal or in a field overlooking potential crossing points.

On Beech Tree Walk Bridge, tank traps remain by the side of the parapet. There are more traps covering the top of the next bridge, which can be seen from Beech Tree Walk and shortly to be passed on the towpath as the walk continues.

The walk continues to Crofton Bridge shortly before Lock 61, which is on the line of a Roman road to Cunetio, near Mildenhall and Marlborough. From here, Crofton Pumping Station is visible and the next section of towpath to Burbage commences.

The lane to Freewarren Bridge next to Sam Farmer Lock (58) offers the nearest canal access when the pumping station is closed, but there is access opposite Lock 60 via a railway underpass footpath through the grounds of the pumping station. The pumping station is best viewed from Lock 60. The towpath climbs imperceptibly to the summit of the canal at Crofton Top Lock (55) past locks 57 and 56.

The lower gates of Lock 62 in 2016. Note the brick treading arc, which allows pressure to be placed on the balance arm of the gate to open it. (SU 269 629)

Left: The rack and pinion sluice gear of Lock 62.

Below: The paddle gear on the bottom gate of Crofton Lock 60.

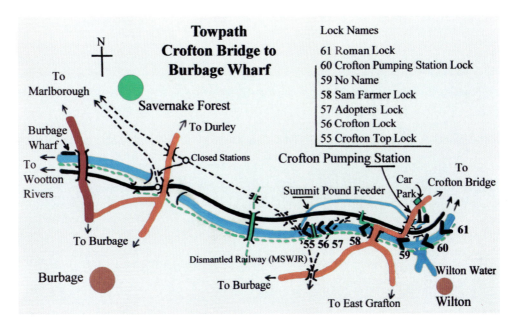

Towpath Crofton Bridge to Burbage Wharf

Lock Names

61 Roman Lock
60 Crofton Pumping Station Lock
59 No Name
58 Sam Farmer Lock
57 Adopters Lock
56 Crofton Lock
55 Crofton Top Lock

There was a good view of Class 47 no. 47145 rumbling past Crofton with a rake of empty stone wagons bound for one of the Somerset quarries on 13 April 1982. The canal and towpath look in a good state of health after being recently restored.

Spotlight on Crofton Pumping Station

A pumping station lifts water from a reservoir or flowing source to the summit level of the canal. This assumes there is no natural source at its summit to keep the canal navigable. Without a replenishing water source at the summit, the water in the canal would slowly drain away in both directions downstream of the summit.

There are two pumping stations on the Kennet and Avon Canal, one at Claverton and the other at Crofton. Crofton was built in 1807 above the summit level of the canal to allow pumped water to flow down a feeder stream, a distance of one mile to the canal's summit at 450ft above sea level in the pound between Lock 55 Crofton Top and Lock 54 at Cadley. The summit pound is 40ft above the level of Lock 60, situated below the pumping station and a reliable water source. To maintain level water in the summit pound, it was necessary to place the canal at Savernake in a cutting and through a tunnel.

The original Crofton structure housed two beam engines – the first Boulton and Watt engine was in use by 1809. A second was operational in 1812. Steam was supplied by three low-pressure Waggon boilers, which operated at 5lb per square inch (psi). The flue for the boilers was rectangular and attached to the wall of the building.

The water supply to the pumps was taken from the pound below Lock 60 and was replenished naturally with spring water. Water from the canal pound was taken through a culvert to a well, where the water was pumped by the engines to discharge into the canal feeder and the summit pound of the canal. By 1836, the spring water supply was inadequate. The situation was resolved by the creation of a reservoir adjacent to the canal, below and opposite the pumping station, called Wilton Water.

The pumping station seen from Lock 60 in 2017. (SU 262 623)

The beam of the 1812 Boulton and Watt beam engine.

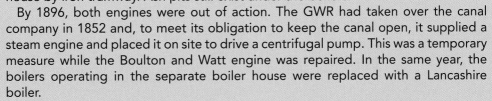

In 1843, Thomas Blackwell, the Kennet and Avon's engineer, contracted Harvey and Company of Hayle in Cornwall to replace the Waggon boilers with Cornish boilers capable of working at 20psi. The higher working pressure necessitated the conversion of the 1812 Boulton and Watt engine. Blackwell also decided to replace the original 1809 engine with a compound double-acting twin cylinder model. The replacement engine was installed in 1846. The higher working pressure of the engine resulted in the installation of a new boiler house with a separate iron chimney. This soon corroded and in 1856 it was replaced with a brick example. The flues from the boilers were connected to the new chimney and the original wall chimney was demolished.

Coal for the boilers was brought in by barge via the Somerset Coal Canal and unloaded at a small wharf below Lock 60. From there, it was moved to the boiler house by iron tramway. Ash pits still exist under the boilers.

By 1896, both engines were out of action. The GWR had taken over the canal company in 1852 and, to meet its obligation to keep the canal open, it supplied a steam engine and placed it on site to drive a centrifugal pump. This was a temporary measure while the Boulton and Watt engine was repaired. In the same year, the boilers operating in the separate boiler house were replaced with a Lancashire boiler.

In 1905, the GWR became involved in rebuilding the Sims patent engine supplied by Harveys in 1846 as a conventional Cornish type with a new 42in bore cylinder. At a similar time, the Cornish boilers in the main building were replaced with a single Lancashire boiler. Engines and boilers continued in operation until 1952. The Boulton and Watt continued a few more years until in 1959 the brick chimney had deteriorated sufficiently to have the top 36ft removed. This affected the fires in the boilers, which failed to draw, with smoke billowing out of the boiler doors. Unable to operate, the boilers and engines were retired.

By now, British Waterways was in control of the canal and pumping station and it was still necessary to raise water to the summit level as the canal was in partial use. At first, a diesel pump was used, followed by electric pumps.

On 14 April 1968, the Kennet and Avon Canal Trust purchased Crofton Pumping Station for the paltry sum of £75. Its objective was to restore the engines and boilers to full working order and the buildings into a fully safe condition. Financial backing was obtained with the help of English Heritage, grants from central and local government and the Manifold Trust, as well as charitable donations.

Above left: The front of the preserved section of the 1896 Lancashire boiler.

Above right: A spare Lancashire boiler is kept in well preserved condition by volunteers and resides adjacent to the boiler water header tank. It is similar to the example in operation inside the boiler house and weighs 20 tons and holds 18 tons of water in service.

To enable the boilers to have any chance of working, the flues required rebuilding after below ground brickwork had collapsed. To cater for the lack of draught after the chimney was reduced in height, a force draughting fan was incorporated in the flue rebuilding. The chimney was eventually rebuilt to full height in 1997. The strength of the chimney is enhanced by adjustable steel waist bands at regular intervals.

Major restoration was required on the boiler in the main boiler house. The Boulton and Watt engine valves were removed and reseated. The rest of the engine was in remarkably good condition. The condenser and pumps required minor restoration. The Harvey engine was also restored and steamed in 1971.

The site is open to the public on specified days between March and October and has special steam-up days throughout the opening period.

The pumping station is Grade 1 listed. The 1812 Boulton and Watt engine is the oldest working beam engine in the world still able to perform its original task in the location it was originally installed.

Also on the Crofton site is a hand-operated Archimedean screw water pump protected in a wooden tiled shelter. The pump consists of an open threaded screw inside a wooden case held together with metal bands. When the screw is turned manually with a cranked handle, water is scooped up in the spiral screw and emptied at the top end. It was used to empty locks before motor-driven pumps were invented.

Right: **The 82ft-high brick chimney was restored to full height in 1997.**

Below: **A 1910 photograph of the pump in action.**

After Crofton, the canal turns in a northwesterly direction, still with the railway following the canal. Lock 57 is called Adopters Lock after the charitable people who adopted a section of waterway in support of its preservation.

Wolfhall Bridge is passed and the banks at each side of the canal steepen. The railway still hugs the canal, but compared to the 1970s it is difficult to appreciate it is still there, as trees and scrub obscure it from view. The banks become increasingly wooded as Bruce Tunnel comes into view.

Over the tunnel portal is a large weather-worn tablet that is now illegible, but a smaller recent replacement has been located at eye level. It reads:

Adopters Lock 57 in 2016. (SU 255 622)

Class 47 no. 47510 on 2 August 1977, going away from my towpath location at Savernake with a West of England express from Paddington. The canal is still and unused, yet not choked with weed, and the towpath is just a narrow track known and walked by locals.

The Kennet and Avon Canal Company inscribe this tunnel with the name BRUCE in testimony of the gratitude for the uniform and effectual support of the Right Honourable Thomas Bruce, Earl of Ailesbury and Charles Lord Bruce his son. Through the whole progress of this great national work by which direct communication by water was opened between the cities of London and Bristol. Anno Domini 1810.

Bruce tunnel was built between 1806 and 1809 and opened to traffic when the Kennet and Avon was officially opened in 1810. It was a condition of passage through Thomas Bruce's estate that a tunnel be built. The tunnel is 502 yards long and had chains attached to the wall to enable barges to be pulled through. Momentum eased the pulling power necessary once the barge or narrowboat was moving forward. The towpath changes to a rising path to a road, which is crossed and the path descends with the railway now directly adjacent to the right-hand side of the path, having crossed the canal over the tunnel.

The footpath from Savernake drops steeply down beside the railway and passes beneath it before the proper towpath and the canal are reached. In autumn, this is a lovely colourful stretch. The towpath is covered in bronze fallen rustling beech leaves. The branches overhang the canal and give the water reflections of yellow, green and gold. A mallard slides by and its wake causes the coloured reflections to dance, here and there catching splashes of blue from the sky. The surface reflections constantly change and distort.

On the approach to Burbage Wharf is one of the best scenes on the Kennet and Avon Canal – the wharf and crane seen through the arch of the bridge. Burbage Wharf was built in 1831 by the Earl of Ailesbury and continued to be used until

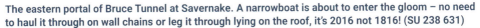

The eastern portal of Bruce Tunnel at Savernake. A narrowboat is about to enter the gloom – no need to haul it through on wall chains or leg it through lying on the roof, it's 2016 not 1816! (SU 238 631)

Above: This scene approaching Burbage was transformed by a golden autumn. As a narrowboat heads out of Burbage towards the western portal of Bruce Tunnel. (SU 226 635)

Left: Burbage Wharf and its crane seen through Burbage Wharf Bridge in late October 2016. (SU 224 635)

shortly before World War Two. The buildings were constructed with locally made bricks and are now dwellings. The building next to the wharf originally had an opening in it for horse-drawn carts to access the canal. It also served as a warehouse for the transit of goods to and from destinations on the canal and the locality.

Incoming goods were coal, probably from the Somerset coalfield, agricultural lime and general merchandise. Outgoing were local bricks, farm produce and timber from Savernake Forest. The wharf is set back, leaving sufficient water for a winding hole, a necessary requirement if carriers had to return on the route.

The most significant feature of the wharf is the preserved wooden crane constructed of green oak. It is the last remaining of its type on the Kennet and Avon Canal. The crane was in use up to c1939 and although still extant in 1972, had deteriorated beyond salvation. Total replacement was necessary if an example of this type of wooden crane was to be preserved for posterity. A group of volunteers under the direction of the Wiltshire Industrial Archaeological Society restored the crane to working order. Unfortunately, without either use or maintenance, its condition again deteriorated. It was subsequently restored into the condition seen today.

The crane was designed to lift two tons and has two counter-balance weights, each weighing one ton. It was constructed around a king post of 2ft diameter. The body of the crane pivots on the top of the king post with a substantial spigot and socket arrangement. It revolves by manual effort through rollers and wheels running against a metal ring at the base of the king post, which also keeps the structure level. Goods are lifted via a simple hand-turned gear wheel and chain.

There is no public parking at the wharf and viewing the crane from the bridge is not recommended due to a narrow, busy and twisting road with no public footpath. Furthermore, there is no towpath access.

The journey from Burbage Wharf towards Wootton Rivers is best tackled from the opposite direction due to lack of access to the towpath at Burbage. There are four locks between Burbage and Wootton Rivers (54–51) in an east–west direction. Lock 54 is named Cadley Lock, which is the end of the summit pound from Crofton.

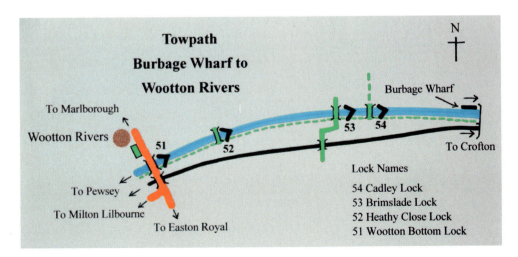

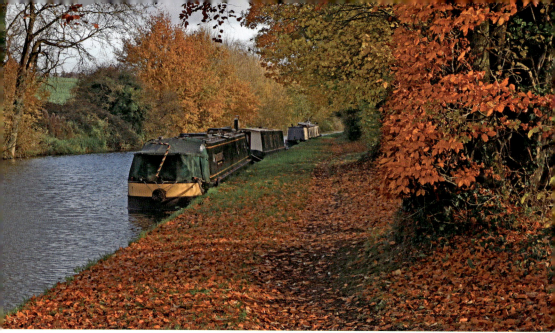

A rich tapestry of autumn shades looking towards Burbage from Heathy Close Lock, November 2016. (SU 202 632)

The convenient parking at Wootton Rivers was used for the next length of towpath to Pewsey at the end of November, which was bright and cold. A complete absence of narrowboats moving on the canal left the water calm and undisturbed.

There are no locks on this level stretch of water, which takes the canal all the way to Devizes, a distance of 12 miles. After an east to west alignment at Burbage, the canal swings west-south-west with landscape views to the north.

Pewsey Wharf is a mile from the centre of the town. The canal no longer has the railway for company, it having slowly veered away towards Pewsey town shortly after Wootton Rivers.

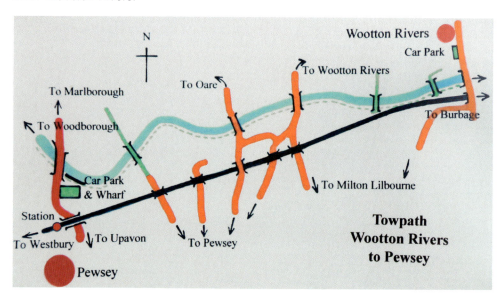

An autumn view over Pewsey Wharf from the A345 road bridge. (SU 158 611)

One of many pill boxes placed at strategic positions along or near the north bank of the canal, seen in November 2016. (SU 168 617)

The view west through the arch of the A345 road bridge at Pewsey in November 2016. (SU 158 611)

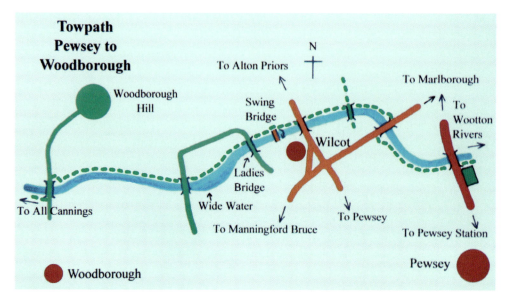

Approaching Bristow Bridge. (SU 151 615)

The next stage from Pewsey to Woodborough was undertaken in the middle of February. Winter wind had dried the towpath a little and walking was easier. There were no narrowboats on the move, but a canoeist was enjoying the calm weather.

The canal sides were quite wooded as bridge 115, Bristow Bridge, was approached. At Bristow Bridge the towpath switches to the north bank of the canal. Passing over the bridge and joining the towpath, the scene looking back through the arch of the bridge was delightful. After passing four more bridges including Wilcot Swing Bridge, the most significant feature on this length of canal, Ladies Bridge and the Wide Water preceding it, was approached. The canal widens sufficiently to give the appearance of a lake, hence its name, Wide Water, an unusual creation on a canal.

The stretch of land through which the canal was planned to pass was owned by Lady Susannah Wroughton of Wilcot Manor. In 1793, she objected to the canal cutting through her land and was believed appeased with a cash settlement of £500, an elaborate bridge with a balustraded parapet at each end and an ornamental lake through which the canal would then be allowed to pass.

Ladies Bridge is dated 1808 and must be attributed to Rennie, engineer of the canal at the time. A footpath from Ladies Bridge leads to Swanborough Tump, about 600 yards south of the canal. Here there is a commemorative stone upon which a plaque reads:

'Here in the year 871 the future King Alfred the Great met his elder brother King Aethelred I on their way to fight the invading Danes and each swore that if the other died in battle the dead man's children would inherit the lands of their father King Aethelwulf.'

Another plaque on the same commemoration stone records that in c850 this was the meeting place of the Hundred [an administrative division] of Swanborough.

At Wilcot, the proposed but never built canal linking the Kennet and Avon with Salisbury would have joined. This was part of a scheme to link Bristol with

Wide Water at Wilcot, east of Ladies Bridge. (SU 130 607)

Southampton. The vista opens out to the north of the canal with views of Picked Hill and Woodborough Hill. At Woodborough Fields Bridge a pair of tank traps, relics of World War Two, required negotiating to access the top of the bridge.

With no parking near Woodborough Fields Bridge, it was necessary to start the next towpath stretch from Honey Street Wharf, which is down a short lane signed to

Ladies Bridge, 8 February 2017. Look for interesting old graffiti on the face of the bridge. (SU 129 607)

A flock of gregarious rooks take flight towards Woodborough Hill. On the slopes are ancient cultivation strips known as strip lynchets.

the Barge Inn. Turn right on the towpath to return to the end of the previous walk at Woodborough Bridge from the opposite direction.

Although it is only a mile to Woodborough, there are three points of interest. From the wharf, the towpath takes us under the minor road to Alton Barnes. Shortly after the bridge, above the moored narrowboats on the distant hills, is Alton Barnes

Tank traps remain in situ on the north sides of Woodborough Fields Bridge. During World War Two there would have been traps over the width of the bridge. In the distance is Woodborough Hill. February 2017. (SU 114 607)

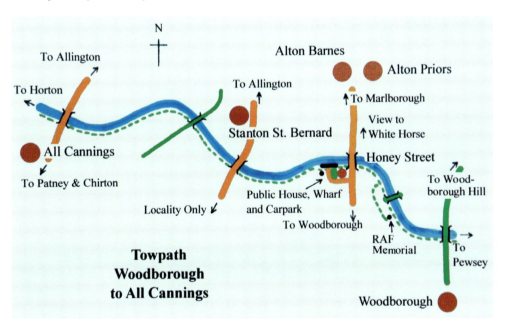

White Horse, one of eight scoured into Wiltshire hillsides. The horse was cut in 1812, only two years after the canal opened, under the direction of farmer Robert Pile. He paid £20 to Jack, the painter, to design and cut the horse, who in turn subcontracted the cutting of the turf and compaction of the chalk to John Harvey. Before the work was finished and unbeknown to John Harvey or Robert Pile, Jack, the painter absconded with the money, failing to pay John Harvey for the sub-contracted work.

After the moorings, the towpath narrows and becomes rutted and muddy in winter, but the next two points of interest are not far away. On the right, there is a sign directing towpath walkers to a memorial to an aircraft crash in 1944. The diversion takes visitors into a field where the crash took place, but before the memorial is reached there is a bridge crossing the canal between fields. Guarding the bridge on the northern side is a pill box with the crossing place in direct sight through a loophole. The bridge also had anti-tank measures – tank traps and spikes. Neither feature was used in anger.

A little further, on the edge of the field that backs on to the canal, there is a rubble stone-built memorial to the crew of an Albermarle bomber while on training duties hauling a Hadrian glider in 1944. The plane took off from RAF Keevil, near Steeple Ashton, and crashed near the site of the memorial. Return to the towpath turning right to complete the short distance to Woodborough Bridge. Then retrace your steps back to the Barge Inn, but continue along the towpath towards All Cannings Bridge to complete the section.

The next stage to Horton starts from All Cannings village. To access All Cannings Bridge at the end of the last stage between Honey Street and All Cannings Bridge, take a right on a byway at the end of the road, which leads to a lane and the bridge.

After Woodway Bridge, Allington Swing Bridge comes into view. This is always kept open for pedestrians; the narrowboats have to open and close it to continue along the canal. An instruction plate on the bridge informs how to operate it. After

The Alton Barnes White Horse is seen over moored narrowboats at Honey Street on the same date. The one pictured is suitably named after the affectionate nickname for Wiltshire folk. (SU 105 615 – location; SU 107 637 – white horse).

Allington Swing Bridge the canal turns south-west, then straightens for a while in a north-westerly direction, followed by a turn to the north-east. All this to follow the contours around a hill called The Knoll.

The landscape opens out, exposing a pill box in the field opposite. The canal narrows slightly to accommodate Horton Fields Swing Bridge, where there is a seat

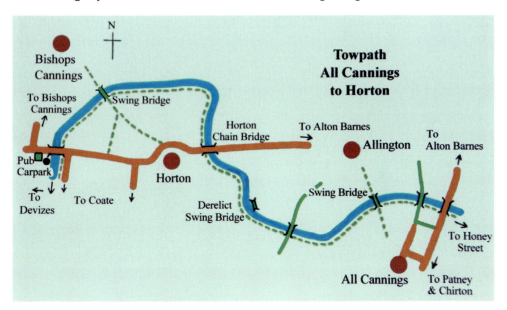

Allington Swing Footbridge photographed in November 2017. (SU 068 626) A footpath crossing serving the villages of Bishops Cannings and Horton.

for a breather. The swing bridge is left open and seems to serve no purpose as there is no footpath or farm track on the opposing bank.

After more contour changes of direction, houseboats start appearing on the towpath bank. The Horton Chain Bridge came into view. The photographic caption for the bridge explains the reason for its name. After the chain bridge, the canal skirts the village in a large loop to the north, before returning the canal south of the road to Devizes.

There is another swing bridge about two-thirds around the Horton loop. This is open to walkers, the narrowboaters having to open, close and secure it after passing through. The path connects Horton and Bishop's Cannings villages. A pillbox on the north bank of the canal is visible.

Above: Horton Fields Swing Bridge is on the opposite bank of the canal to the towpath (SU 056 627).

Below left and below right: Horton Chain Bridge and iron ring fixed to the inside of the arch, presumably there were others, which are no longer present. I believe the bridge is so named because chains through the iron rings pulled up a stop gate from the bottom of the canal to allow the section to be drained, as there is a very long pound without locks between Wootton Rivers and Devizes. (SU 053 634)

Bishops Cannings' Swing Bridge. (SU 044 638)

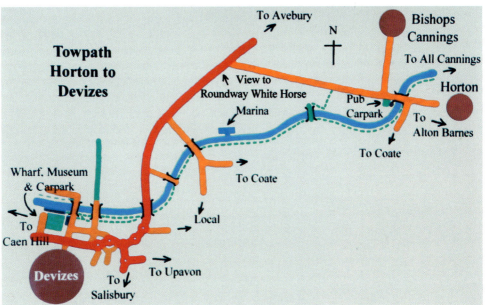

The end of this section's walk is at Horton Bridge, where the bridge has the Bridge Inn for company.

Starting the next towpath stage to Devizes can be incredibly muddy in winter. However, beyond the next bridge the path improves and eventually turns to tarmac as it approaches Devizes Wharf. Prior to reaching the solid footing there is a view of the Devizes (Roundway Hill) white horse, seen above the narrowboats in Devizes Marina. Unfortunately, the Le Marchant Barracks building is partially obscured by housing.

From Devizes Wharf the stretch of towpath towards Seend Cleeve takes in the famous Devizes flight of locks, which is reviewed in more detail later. The old, bonded wharf warehouse at Devizes, where goods were stored before duty was paid, is now the headquarters of the Kennet and Avon Canal Trust, with a museum about the history and restoration of the canal situated over the offices. The large brick warehouse at the side of the canal is now a theatre.

Devizes Marina with the Devizes white horse on the hillside beyond at Roundway in February 2018. (SU 025 624)

The towpath switches sides at Cemetery Road Bridge and is on the opposite bank to the wharf, providing a good overall impression of its size when it was in full use in the 19th century. The Devizes to Westminster Canoe Race, which takes place every Easter, starts here.

On the right, after a number of moored boats, a footpath rises to a road. On the corner overlooking the canal is another pill box, with no interior access. Further on, we reach Town Bridge and Lock 50, named Kennet Lock after Kennet District Council. On the opposite bank, there is a horse arch under the road near the canal lock, which took a horse-drawn tramway under the bridge (see 'Spotlight' on the Caen Hill flight of locks).

The towpath switches sides again at Town Bridge to take the path of the horse tramway. Kennet Lock is the start of the Devizes flight of 29 locks, which drops the canal 237 feet in two miles at an average gradient of 1 in 44. There are six locks before the main descent at Caen Hill and seven after, the flight ending at Lock 22, Lower Foxhangers.

The canal widens before the main flight to accommodate a greater supply of water. The main highway through Devizes crosses the canal again at Prison Bridge, so named after the prison built here shortly after 1810 and demolished in 1927.

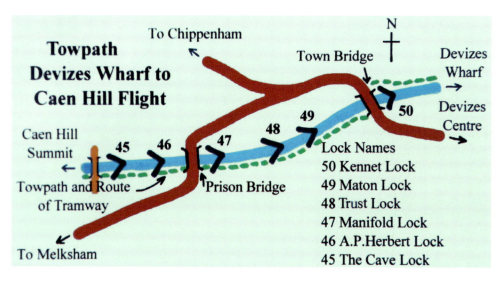

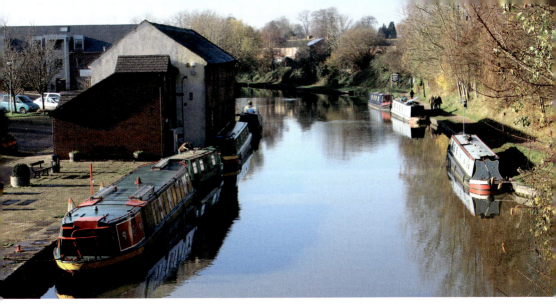

Above: Devizes Wharf looking west. (SU 005 618)

Right: A moored narrowboat outside The Black Horse pub. (ST 995 616)

Below: Prison Bridge. The towpath takes the route of the old horse tramway under the road. This conveniently meant that in the days of horse-drawn barges the horse did not have to climb up and over the road to reach the towpath on the other side. It is almost a tunnel rather than a bridge, but momentum would have taken the boat through. (ST 993 615)

Spotlight on the Caen Hill Flight

John Rennie, engineer for the Kennet and Avon Canal, must have pondered how to overcome the sharp change in contours west of Devizes. Banking works and aqueducts were an option, which would have involved veering off the present course, following different contours, but eventually the same drop in canal level would have been required, over greater distance with expensive civil engineering works. The most appropriate option was a flight of 16 locks in quick succession. In order for the flight to work efficiently, it was necessary to construct 15 side pounds, the first below Lock 44 and the last below Lock 28, in effect between locks 28 and 29. This was to hold large reservoirs of spare water to feed the locks.

The Devizes flight of locks was the last part of the canal to be completed. It was opened below Foxhangers and from the east into Devizes before 1810. For through traffic, it was necessary to build an iron railroad connecting both ends of the unfinished canal. Hence the towpath arches in the bridges where the iron railroad passed under the roads. Barges needed to be unloaded at each end and their contents placed on trucks on the horse-drawn iron railroad for transfer up or down the canal route, then loaded into barges again at the other end.

A huge number of bricks was required to build the staircase of lock chambers. Brick clay was naturally occurring halfway up the intended flight of locks on the south side of the route. This resource was used in a specially built brickworks to supply the requirements of the civil engineers, who not only required bricks for the locks, but a vast quantity for Bruce Tunnel at Savernake. The building of the tunnel and consequent shortage of bricks delayed work on the Caen Hill lock chambers.

The Caen Hill Lock flight photographed in 1995. The balance arm of the gate of Lock 28 in the foreground is welded at the end and made of steel. The wide water at the base of the main flight is a winding hole. (ST 978 615)

Between 1829 and 1843 the flight was gas lit, using locally made gas. There was a charge for using the flight of locks during gas-lit hours – one shilling per barge and less for a smaller boat. Clearly the flight was being used during the hours of darkness. It must have been busy in the first half of the 19th century, until railways started sapping trade. The influence of the railways must have been significant in turning the lights out.

The Caen Hill flight seen in the winter of 1904. The photograph was taken from above the chamber of Lock 28. The level of water looks high in the winding hole at the bottom of the flight, which, I suppose, also served as the 16th side pound.

Lock 44 and the Lock Keepers Cottage at the top of the flight in 1905.

It took up to six hours to navigate all the Devizes locks, depending on the traffic. There must have been a queue of barges and boats awaiting passage at each end of the main flight in the 1820s and '30s.

By 1880, the side pounds started silting up, partially because of steam boats swishing silt from their props into the pounds. Trade on the canal continued to decline and by 1947 the side pounds were choked with weeds, and there was little incentive to dredge them. The last cargo through the flight was in 1948, a load of grain from Avonmouth to Newbury. In 1951, the flight was declared unsafe and all the lock gates were padlocked.

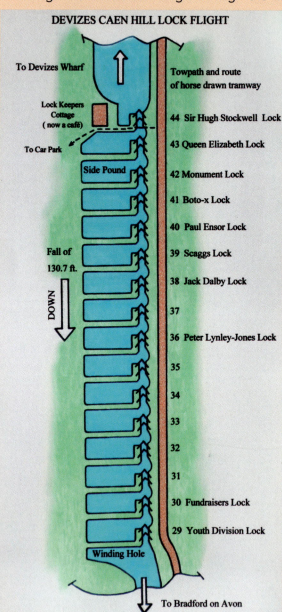

DEVIZES CAEN HILL LOCK FLIGHT

To Devizes Wharf

Towpath and route of horse drawn tramway

Lock Keepers Cottage (now a café)

To Car Park

Side Pound

Fall of 130.7 ft.

DOWN

44 Sir Hugh Stockwell Lock

43 Queen Elizabeth Lock

42 Monument Lock

41 Boto-x Lock

40 Paul Ensor Lock

39 Scaggs Lock

38 Jack Dalby Lock

37

36 Peter Lynley-Jones Lock

35

34

33

32

31

30 Fundraisers Lock

29 Youth Division Lock

Winding Hole

To Bradford on Avon

The flight fell into dereliction, the lock gates slowly rotted and disintegrated, and ironwork began to rust and seize up. On the positive side, it began to be a haven for flora and fauna, but looked untidy and forlorn.

Since the formation of the Kennet and Avon Canal Trust in 1962, the opening of the complete canal was paramount, but Caen Hill presented a daunting task. In 1977, a scheme was sponsored jointly between Kennet District Council and the British Waterways Board for restoration of the complete Devizes flight of 29 locks. The sum of money involved was £175,000, but this did not include replacement of the lock gates.

In 2017, passages were allowed through the flight from 1 April to 15 September between 8am and 5pm. From 16 to 30 September, between 8am and 4pm and from 1 October to 31 March between 8am and 1pm. All traffic had to be clear three hours after the last entry time. The timings suggest it takes a little less than three hours to negotiate the 16 locks – not long really.

Looking down the flight In May 1981 when derelict.

On the same day looking up the flight. The side pounds were bogs.

Above and below: **An interesting comparison looking up to the top lock (44) of the flight in 1910 and 19 January 2017. (ST 988 615)**

Looking down the flight from Lock 39 in January 2017. In the right foreground is the entrance to one of the side pounds. (ST 987 615)

When the flight was gas lit between 1829 and 1843, the lock keeper was responsible for collecting tolls for craft to negotiate the flight during the hours of darkness.

In the photographs of the derelict canal in 1981, time and money has been spent on the restoration of the lock entry brickwork and capstones. Closer views of the capstones of the actual lock chambers show considerable depression wear from bargees' boots treading to and fro, seeing their vessels safely through each lock.

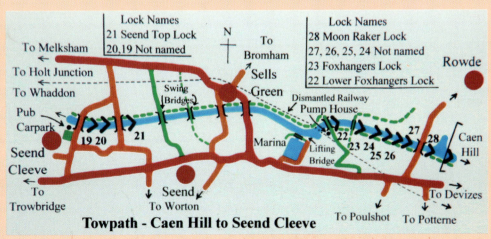

An appeal was raised by the Kennet and Avon Canal Trust to raise £300,000, the estimated cost of new lock gates. There was a choice of materials – wood or steel. It was known that wooden gates had a definitive lifespan before they needed replacement, roughly in the region of 25 years.

Steel, on the other hand, stands the test of time much better and bearing in mind that a production run of 116 individual gates would be required, was very much cheaper. The lock gate balance arm of a steel gate is usually rounded and a prominent weld line is seen at the juncture of the shape. Two years after my 1981 photographs of the flight were taken, the side pounds were dug out and restored.

Seen from the air, the Caen Hill flight looks like a giant's staircase. This is the most impressive canal feature in Wiltshire, if not in the whole of England. For those visiting by car, there is limited parking at the base of the flight on a small lane connecting the A361 with the village of Rowde. There is also a car park for the flight along the lane. This takes visitors to the top of the flight, but the most impressive view is from Lock 28 beyond the base of the flight.

Since restoration of the flight, narrowboat traffic continues to increase in the summer and it is wise for bargees to book passage through the locks to avoid long delays.

Traffic increase also results in the use of more water, with gates opening and closing frequently. To counter this effect, a return pump was installed at Foxhangers in 1996, which is capable of returning seven million gallons of water per day to the top of the flight.

Lock 22 at Lower Foxhangers, the end of the Devizes flight of locks. (ST 966 616) The towpath changes canal banks on the other side of the bridge. The building roof seen over the bridge parapet is the pumping station, which can pump the equivalent of one lock full every 11 minutes.

We left the Caen Hill flight behind after taking the old tramway arch under Marsh Lane Bridge immediately after Lock 28. There is access from the lane after the tramway arch tunnel under the road. Here there is more evidence from World War Two, two tank traps.

Restarting the walk after the main flight, there were six more locks to pass on foot before the complete Devizes flight ended. The canal is wide before Lock 26, where there is a blind canal inlet with a small spit of land separating it from the lock. At Lower Foxhangers, there is a pumping station to return water to the top of Caen Hill and here the towpath changes sides of the canal to take the north bank.

Beyond Lower Foxhangers, the erstwhile Devizes branch crossed the canal. The bridge cutwaters still exist and the embankment opposite clearly shows the route of the railway. (The term 'cutwater' describes the shape of the bridge supports between the arches. Generally, a pointed shape allows water to flow past the bridge smoothly without disturbance. This more commonly applies to rivers, but also applies to canals when the wash from a passing boat causes turbulence.) Here is a marina and boatyard, with the entrance to the marina under a lifting bridge on the opposite bank.

At Martinslade Bridge, the canal changes orientation to face more southwesterly through Sells Green. There are always houseboats near centres of population and such was the case at Sells Green. Smoke was wafting from a series of narrowboat chimneys moored at the side of the cut.

We were now approaching Seend Cleeve and The Barge Inn, a very popular canalside venue and the end of the longer towpath stretch from Devizes Wharf. This length may be shortened by breaking the walk at the bottom of the main Devizes flight and returning to the Wharf. There is a suitable roadside lay-by to restart the walk to Seend Cleeve at the base of the main flight.

Seend Cleeve was the location for the Seend Ironworks. Iron ore had been mined here long before it was decided to commercially exploit the site in c1850. Initially

Just beyond the pumping station at Lower Foxhangers, the former Patney and Chirton to Holt Junction railway line traversed the canal. The bridge piers and cutwaters are still in situ. Out of view to the right of the picture is a marina with a lifting bridge to cross the entrance. (ST 965 617)

the ore was transported by barge to Bristol for onward shipment to Welsh smelters. In 1857, smelters were built on the site, but a rail connection added in the same year took the mineral trade from the canal. The business wasn't profitable and smelting ceased *c*1876 and the smelters were demolished in 1889. However, ore continued to be mined until 1946.

The Sells Green Footbridge is kept in the open footway position, narrowboats needing to open and close it after their passage. (ST 945 617)

The Seend Iron Works at Seend Cleeve *c*1860. The smelters were built in 1857, but by this time there was a rail connection to the Devizes railway branch line and this would have been used to transport minerals in preference to the canal. (ST 932 614)

Just over half a mile after restarting the towpath at Seend Cleeve, the canal takes a dogleg to the southwest before resuming its westerly course towards Semington.

A number of swing bridges and a modern aqueduct over the A350 are encountered before approaching locks 16 and 15 at Semington. Below Lock 15, Buckley's Lock, is a small wharf followed by a winding hole, which was created when the entrance to the Wilts & Berks Canal was sealed off. The Wilts & Berks entrance is marked on the face of the modified old towpath bridge over the canal entrance. A mile and a quarter further and we reached Whaddon Bridge, the end of this section and the start of the next to Bradford on Avon.

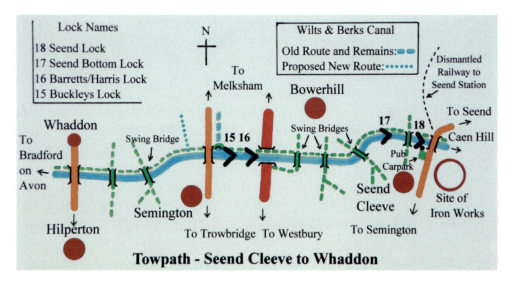

Lock Names
18 Seend Lock
17 Seend Bottom Lock
16 Barretts/Harris Lock
15 Buckleys Lock

N

Wilts & Berks Canal
Old Route and Remains:
Proposed New Route:

Dismantled Railway to Seend Station

To Melksham

Bowerhill

To Seend

Whaddon

Swing Bridge

15 16

Swing Bridges

17 18

Caen Hill

To Bradford on Avon

Pub Carpark

Seend Cleeve

Site of Iron Works

Hilperton

Semington

To Trowbridge To Westbury

To Semington

Towpath - Seend Cleeve to Whaddon

The one-time entrance to the Wilts and Berks Canal at Semington is marked on the stone face of the old bridge over the canal, seen in the centre of the photograph. (ST 900 610)

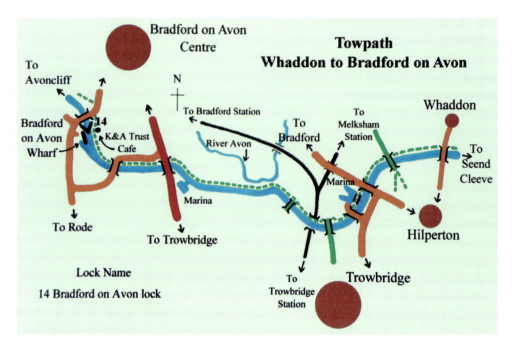

Hilperton Marina. (ST 859 600)

Stop gates under Hilperton Marina access bridge. (ST 858 598)

Recommencing at Whaddon Bridge, the scene was tranquil until we reached Hilperton Marina. On the south bank of the canal there are many hire boats moored. There is also access for boats into a modern developed marina on the north side of the canal. The towpath traverses the marina entrance via a bridge. A modern road access bridge crosses the canal, under which a pair of stop gates is tucked into the banks.

After the Marina, the canal resumes its westerly course outside Trowbridge to reach Bradford on Avon. I had in my photographic collection a Kennet and Avon Canal scene dated c1910, said to be taken at Trowbridge. I had pinpointed the probable position on an Ordnance Survey map by the long straight stretch of canal, followed by a curve in the cut in the foreground of the picture. Comparing scenes more than 100 years apart, there is a new bridge in the distance for the marina and the trees and shrubbery on the right-hand side hide industrial units beyond the marina. Needless to say, I stopped at the aqueduct over the Weymouth to Bristol line at Bradford South Junction for a breather and a short spell of railway photography.

There were not many narrowboats taking leisure time on the canal that day, but at Widbrook Bridge a photographic opportunity presented itself with one chugging towards Bradford. It was at Widbrook where the ill-fated Dorset and Somerset Canal would have joined the K&A, probably in c1810. We passed a pillbox and soon Bradford wharf came into view.

The canal at Bradford on Avon is much higher than the town, which nestles at each side of the river Avon, following the contours to limit the number of locks required to a single example at the end of the wharf and next to the road bridge. The road takes a tortuous twist to cross the canal at this point and the towpath is non-existent at the bridge, so the busy road has to be crossed to access it again some 20 yards or so down the hill by the Canal Tavern.

The water is wide here to accommodate the wharf and its business, albeit no longer trading in goods, but in pleasure, a fair number of holiday narrowboats is moored here.

Following the opening of the canal in 1810, the Upper Wharf developed into an important distribution centre between Bath and London. There were storage and distribution facilities. From its inception to the middle of the 19th century, the wharf was one of the busiest locations on the canal.

Decline set in after 1860, when once again, the railway was to blame for loss of trade, it being far cheaper and quicker to transport minerals, grain and general goods by rail.

There is always plenty of activity at the wharf and lock, if only serving as a canal holiday starting point and a mooring, sometimes two abreast, for a lunch break. There is no better place to be a gongoozler. The old lock-keeper's cottage is a Kennet and Avon Canal Trust café.

Bradford on Avon is a suitable break point in the walk, leaving the next stage to reach Avoncliff. There are no locks to negotiate for the remainder of the journey through Wiltshire.

Above and below: The canal on the outskirts of Trowbridge, taken in 1910, compared to the same location in 2018. (ST 856 595)

At Bradford on Avon, the Tithe Barn is Grade I listed and is an English Heritage property managed by the Bradford and Avon Heritage Trust. The barn was built in 1340 and used by the Grange, an outlying farm of Shaftesbury Abbey. The Abbey was dissolved in 1539 and the Grange became a farm, but with the major asset of one of the best tithe barns in the United Kingdom. Entry is free at appropriate times.

It is less than 1½ miles from Bradford to Avoncliff. The railway runs parallel with the canal and views of the line can be achieved here and there through the trees. On the way, Bradford Swing Bridge and footbridge are passed.

The aqueduct at Avoncliff is soon reached and the canal turns at right angles to go over both the river Avon and the Wessex main line. There is a footpath across the aqueduct on the eastern side, which gives access to Avoncliff station. The towpath changes sides before the aqueduct is crossed and this can be reached via a service

Situated adjacent to the towpath and half sunk into the ground is this pill box at Bradford on Avon. (ST 826 599)

Towpath - Bradford on Avon to Avoncliff

road under the aqueduct. Here, there is a pub with a terraced garden called the Cross Guns, an ideal spot to take a break for refreshment. On certain days, a nearby café is open.

There are options on the route to return to Bradford on both sides of the canal by taking paths through Barton Farm Country Park or woodland.

The final length of towpath in Wiltshire is from Avoncliff Aqueduct to Dundas Aqueduct, after which is the junction for the truncated remains of the Somerset

Above left: Bradford on Avon Tithe Barn viewed from the rear and as seen from the towpath. (ST 823 604)

Above right: Bradford Swing Bridge is for traffic to and from a sewage pumping station. The footbridge is used to access the south bank of the canal for opening and closing the bridge. There is also a public footpath from here through Barton Farm Country Park and woodland to reach Avoncliff as an alternative route. (ST 813 601)

Below: A narrowboat breaks the tranquility, chugging through a wooded section of the canal near Avoncliffe. (ST 807 601)

Avoncliff Aqueduct seen from the east. The arch on the right is used by the railway, the centre for the river Avon and the left arch allows foot and vehicle access to the opposite side of the canal. Note the bow in the centre of the parapet. (ST 805 600)

Coal Canal. The 110yd-long aqueduct at Avoncliffe was built by John Rennie and engineer John Thomas between 1797 and 1801. They used locally quarried stone, which was prone to fracture in frost, causing buttresses to collapse and requiring continual repairs. The prone parts of the aqueduct were rebuilt in Bath stone, giving more stability. The central span suffered from sagging and needed rebuilding a number of times. The sag is still present today, but during restoration in 1980, the canal was cradled in concrete.

The parapet of the aqueduct is a wonderful viewing point for railway observation and photography, particularly from the Bath direction and the approaching curve to the station. On the opposite bank, as the canal takes a right-angle curve to continue its westerly course, is a pill box. Look closely at the loophole, there may be someone spying on you!

Of all the walks on the towpath in Wiltshire, the stretch between Avoncliff and Dundas aqueducts has to be my favourite. The towpath is well cared for and the woodland on the north bank is lush. It's October and the autumn colours are yet to show their true splendour, but it is beautiful, nevertheless.

The canal twists and turns, eventually to take a northerly course for the remainder of the journey through Wiltshire. Muirhill is soon reached, where there is a wharf on the opposite bank. An information board on the towpath bank describes the scene. Look carefully and a track for iron-wheeled carts can be seen. A quarry at the top of the hill despatched stone by horse-drawn drams to the wharf for loading on to boats.

Also, look for a GWR milepost, rather beaten up, with '68' painted on the surface. This represented 68 miles to Reading and the Thames. There are at least three such examples hereabouts.

The view over Avoncliff taken from the hillside above the canal, *c*1904. The central arch of the aqueduct appears to be strengthened with wooden struts. Note the quarry railway over the aqueduct.

A narrowboat cruises over Avoncliff Aqueduct on its way to Bradford on Avon. There is an obvious sag on the aqueduct clearly seen below the top horizontal rail of the white railings. (ST 804 600)

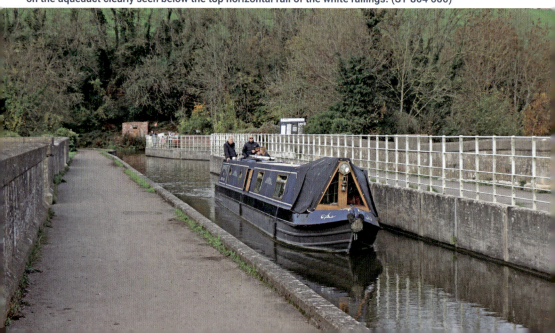

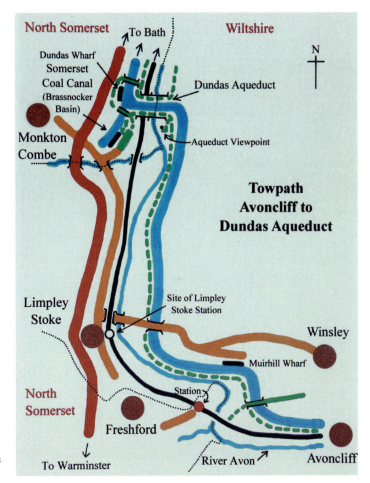

North Somerset

Wiltshire

To Bath

Dundas Wharf
Somerset
Coal Canal
(Brassnocker
Basin)

Dundas Aqueduct

Monkton
Combe

Aqueduct Viewpoint

N

Towpath
Avoncliff to
Dundas Aqueduct

Limpley
Stoke

Site of Limpley
Stoke Station

Winsley

Muirhill Wharf

North
Somerset

Station

Freshford

To Warminster

River Avon

Avoncliff

Below: Autumn colours begin to show in October 2017. A narrowboat approaches Winsley Bridge heading for Dundas Aqueduct. (ST 798 602)

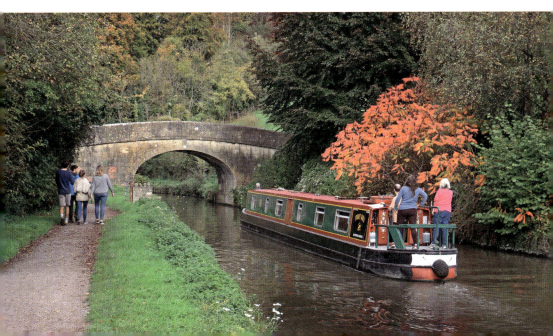

Left: Milepost near Muirhill Wharf. Now a rare survivor on the Kennet and Avon, this is a wooden block bolted to a length of broad-gauge track. They were placed here after the GWR took over the canal and register the distance from Reading in miles with I, II, or III to indicate quarter divisions. (ST 795 605 and ST 792 606)

Below: Muirhill Wharf and plateway track, both on the offside of the canal. (ST 795 605)

Opposite: An idyllic canal scene near Limpley Stoke. (ST 785 623)

A narrowboat crosses Dundas Aqueduct named after Charles Dundas, Chairman of the Kennet and Avon Canal from its inception. (ST 785 625)

The wharf at Dundas in the parish of Monkton Combe. Note the iron crane. (ST 784 625)

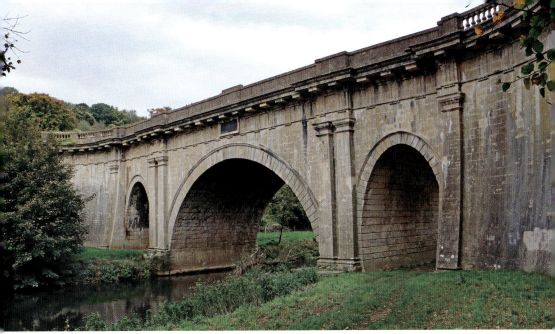

It is not possible to appreciate Dundas Aqueduct without observing it at river level. This view was achieved by taking steps down to the river on the Wiltshire end of the aqueduct. (ST 786 625)

The pound between Bradford on Avon Lock 14 as far as Dundas aqueduct has, since original construction, been liable to landslips by nature of its hillside course above the river Avon and the geology of the area. One of the problems is the rock formation upon which the canal has been cut – oolite, a cemented granular structured rock within which fissures exist. In extreme prolonged wet weather, water permeates into the rock, forcing up air under pressure, which bursts through the bed of the canal. Water leaks from the canal into the surrounding substrate, which loosens, causing landslides and collapse of the canal.

This section, in its derelict state, was known as 'the dry section'. The canal bed, including over the Dundas Aqueduct, required re-lining with polythene and concrete. This treatment will, hopefully, prevent any further canal bed disturbance for the foreseeable future. The work was completed by 1984.

We were walking through a beautiful stretch of slightly meandering canal (once the dry section), no doubt following the contours of the hillside, but now heading in a northerly direction following the Avon valley. There is no hint of Dundas Aqueduct on its approach, until a sharp turn of the canal to the left opens out to the transit of the canal across the valley.

The 150-yard-long aqueduct was built by John Rennie in Bath stone between 1797 and 1801 and opened for traffic in 1805. The county boundary runs through the centre of the river Avon and hence through the middle of the aqueduct, such that the eastern half is in Wiltshire and the western half in the historic county of Somerset (now Avon). Above the central arch and facing south is a bronze plaque dedicated to Charles Dundas, Chairman of the Kennet and Avon Canal Company and dated 1828.

Adjacent to the Somerset Coal Canal entrance is a wharf with an iron crane by Acramans of Bristol. The basin and wharf area also serves as a winding hole. Close by is Brassnocker Basin on the Somerset Coal Canal, where there is a cafe, information centre and car park.

Chapter 7

The Wilts & Berks Canal in Wiltshire

In 1793, Robert and William Whitworth, father and son, surveyed a route for a canal that would allow coal to be shipped from the Somerset coal fields along the Somerset Coal Canal to the towns of Wiltshire and Berkshire, accessing the Thames waterway between Abingdon and Wallingford, eventually reaching London.

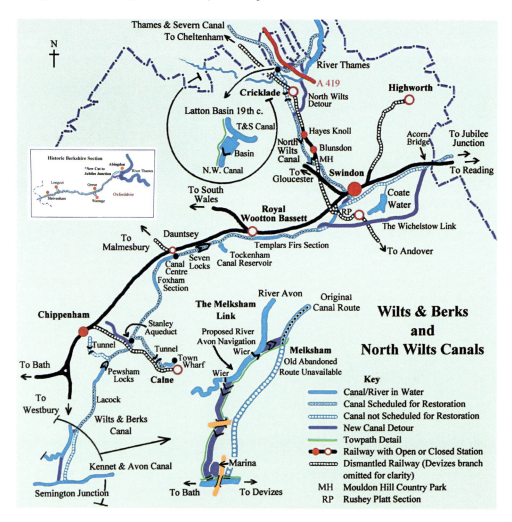

The final line of the canal was chosen to bypass Chippenham and Calne, but branch routes of 1.6 and 3 miles respectively, were planned to reach these towns. Two other short branches over the Wiltshire border in Berkshire on the chosen route to Abingdon were at Longcot and Wantage. Boundary changes in 1974 transferred this part of Berkshire into Oxfordshire.

An Act of Parliament was passed in 1795, giving the construction of the canal Royal Assent. The Act provided for the canal, named the Wilts & Berks, to raise £111,900 equal to 1,119 shares of £100 each. A further Act during construction was passed in 1801 to provide further finance amounting to £200,000 to complete the canal.

Work started at the junction with the Kennet & Avon at Semington in 1796. The canal was completed in 1810 with an opening ceremony at Abingdon, but a further Act of Parliament was necessary to amend the original planned toll rates. Furthermore, during the construction, debts had mounted, making it necessary to require another Act of Parliament in 1815 to raise £100,000 to clear those in turn.

Brickyards were built along the route of the canal as it progressed. It was fortunate that there was an abundance of Kimmeridge clay, practically end to end. The first kilns were built at Melksham,

The blocked entrance to the Wilts & Berks Canal at Semington, in 2017. The old route will remain blocked, despite a target of restoring the canal to its original state. A new junction will be constructed with the Kennet and Avon Canal 100 yards or so to the west of the old junction. Part of the old route shortly after the junction can still be traced for less than half a mile, but it is derelict and overgrown. (Old junction – ST 900 610. New junction – ST 899 610)

Semington junction in 1904, showing the junction of the Wilts & Berks Canal, under the bridge on the left, with the Kennet & Avon Canal. Semington Lock is in the middle distance.

followed by Pewsham, Stanley, and others regularly spaced as the need arose. The last bricks baked in each kiln were used to build the kilns of the next, as the canal construction progressed.

The canal was 52 miles long with six miles of branches. In total, 42 locks were necessary on the mainline, with another three on the Calne branch. The locks were designed to take narrow boats 72ft long and 7ft wide. The canal's water supply was always a problem. A reservoir was provided at Tockenham at the summit pound of the canal, but in 1822 a much larger supply of water was established by diverting the river Cole and creating Coate Water, east of Swindon town.

After the canal was abandoned, this attractive lake was retained as a pleasure park, having a diving board, later improved as a concrete art deco structure. Swimming is no longer allowed in the lake, but the diving structure, which is Grade II listed, has been retained. The park is now called Coate Water Country Park and includes naturalist and author Richard Jeffries' house.

The canal's heyday was in the 1820s, '30s and early '40s. During the latter part of this period, it was ironically used to carry construction materials for the Great Western Railway. With the opening of the railway line to Bristol in 1841 and further rapid railway growth in the subsequent decade, the canal's fortunes rapidly declined.

In 1874, there was a demand to close the canal due to the amount of trade taken by the railway. In 1875, a Bill was prepared for the sale of the canal. In the event that no buyer was forthcoming, the canal would be closed. A consortium of names associated with the canal, together with a Bristol solicitor, rescued the canal in the name of the Wilts, Somerset and Berks Canal Traders Association.

The rescue failed to improve the prosperity of the canal, particularly as the canal was silting up in many places and lighter loads were advisable to avoid grounding. Toll receipts dropped, mainly because the canal east of Swindon to Abingdon was seldom used. Most of the remaining business occurred between Swindon and Semington, with coal and timber predominating.

In 1901, Stanley Aqueduct was breached, emptying a pound of water. The poorly maintained lock gates upstream no doubt lost water from the adjoining pound, adding to the problem. This prevented any through traffic, heralding a further decline in trade. It was uneconomical to repair the breach so the canal slowly fell into neglect and was officially abandoned by an Act of Parliament in 1914.

With the abandonment notice came subsequent dereliction and the line of the canal became overgrown; lock gates rotted and fell apart and the remaining channel narrowed with encroaching

Tockenham reservoir near the summit pound of the canal in 2016. (SU 038 813)

Coate Water Country Park and its listed diving board in 2016. This large additional reservoir serviced the canal with water from 1822 until the canal was abandoned. (SU 177 826)

undergrowth. Stretches of the canal were built upon, particularly in Swindon. In some places, the canal was filled in, while in others, rural pockets of shallow water-filled canal remained.

In 1977, the first signs of restoration of the canal stirred with the formation of the Wilts and Berks Amenity Group, soon after changed to the Wilts and Berks Canal Trust. The overall aim of the Trust is to restore the canal as a recreational resource and wildlife corridor for local communities and visitors. Much has been achieved since the Trust was formed. Major challenges exist, which will require enduring effort from Trust members, public and landowner support in progressive attitudes, manpower and financial assistance.

Beyond Semington, the canal bed is totally overgrown on the approach to Melksham, but is built over in Melksham.

A completely new cut is necessary to recreate the new canal, leading from the Kennet & Avon, and located about 100 yards further to the west of the old entrance. There are plans for a marina at the entrance junction, which will involve creating an overbridge to take the Kennet & Avon towpath over the entrance of the Wilts & Berks.

Detailed route plans have been submitted for environmental and planning issues to be resolved, which will join the new line of the canal to the river Avon, creating a navigation through Melksham town. Seven locks will be required, two of them in the Avon, starting from the new junction at Semington, through open countryside to reach the river Avon, subsequently to leave the Avon to join the original route north of Melksham.

The bridge over the river Avon in Melksham in 2016. A navigation could be created through one of the arches, a major benefit as the bridge would not need to be rebuilt. (ST 904 641)

Land has since been purchased near Queenfield Farm on the northern edge of Melksham, with landowner permission to access adjoining fields. This allows the Trust to work on almost a mile of the former canal through an open landscape. This project has been labelled 'Destination Lacock'.

The remains of the canal were used as demolition excercises in World War Two, making the restoration of it, the locks and buildings all the more difficult.

The top lock of the Pewsham flight under restoration in July 2018. (ST 937 711)

The remains of Pewsham dry dock near the bottom lock of three unrestored in 2018. (ST 937 709)

The flight of three locks, two basins, a dry dock and associated buildings at Pewsham are being restored. The top lock is under the Heritage Heroes Project funded by the People's Postcode Lottery, which offers injured or sick ex-service personnel a chance to gain new skills. Below the bottom lock, a spill weir and a section of canal and towpath of 1,310 yards in length heading towards Lacock has been restored. The flight of locks drops the canal 29 feet.

Above: The Wilts & Berks Canal is marked where the A4 crosses the route of the canal at Pewsham. (ST 946 717)

Right: Evidence of the Chippenham branch near Pewsham Way. (ST 932 8715

With regard to the Chippenham branch of the canal – there are some visible traces, but much has been built over, including a section under Pewsham Way and a tunnel. The old wharf at the end of the canal is now a bus station. Restoration is probably a long way off and a new route will be necessary north-east of the present remains, partially following the old route of the Calne railway branch.

Between the Chippenham branch and the Calne branch is the site of Stanley Aqueduct over the river Marden, the breach of which sounded the death knell for the canal in 1901.

There is water in the town end of the Calne branch and the town wharf has been commemorated with a blue heritage plaque. Calne Lock still exists but has been filled in and holds a barge; it is part of Castlefields Park.

Calne Lock from an engraving c1840.

A preserved section of canal at Calne looking towards the main line 2½ miles distant. The surface of the water is covered in floating plants called azola and duckweed. Photograph taken in 2018. (ST 994 709)

Calne Wharf in 2016. (ST 998 708)

The preserved Calne Lock in Castlefields Park, seen in 2018. (ST 997 708)

Between Pewsham and Dauntsey, a 770-yard section has been restored at Foxham. There is water in the canal at Dauntsey for 770 yards and the lock appears in reasonable condition except there were metal strut supports preventing inward collapse when I viewed the remains in 2017. Planning permission has been granted at Dauntsey for a Canal centre.

Some lock restoration has taken place between Dauntsey and Royal Wootton Bassett on the seven-lock rise, but much work is necessary to restore the canal through this rise to the summit pound at Tockenham. At Wootton Bassett, Templars Firs, there is a 1,250-yard length of restored canal. This is an idyllic length of canal and an example of how the Wilts & Berks Canal will look like in the future.

Above: A restored, but locked lifting bridge at Foxham at the start of a restored section of canal. (ST 980 776)

Right: The canal at Dauntsey with the surface covered in duckweed, showing no water movement in 2017. (ST 995 802)

The lock at Dauntsey in 2017. (ST 996 802)

The restored canal at Templars Firs, Royal Wootton Bassett. (SU 074 816 typical)

Believed to be Lock 3 of the seven-lock rise. (SU 021 807)

When the M4 motorway was built, it severed the canal route. To continue the restored route, a tunnel will be necessary under the motorway – a major obstacle that will cause some disruption to motorway traffic. Once the canal is north of the motorway, a new route for the main line will be necessary skirting south and east of Swindon, retaining part of the old main line as a southern extension to the North Wilts Canal, for which there are also plans for restoration.

Restoration has already taken place through Westleaze and Rushey Platt up to Kingshill. The remaining old main line formation through Swindon has been built over. A new canal must be built, extending the truncated remains at Kingshill to meet the southern end of the North Wilts route near the old junction with the main line. A new route is believed to be feasible through the town. East of this point, the old main line will remain buried under construction or stay abandoned up to the point where the new southern Swindon canal bypass joins the old route east of Swindon at Acorn Bridge.

The landing stage on the canal. (SU 135 830)

The restored old main line at Westleaze looking towards Rushey Platt. (SU 135 830)

The new main line of the Wilts & Berks Canal on the edge of the development at East Wichel looking west and east respectively. (SU 144 824)

Skew bridge taking the erstwhile MSWJR over the canal at Rushey Platt. In 2018, the end of the present watered section was a little further at Kingshill. (SU 137 835)

Some work has been carried out on the new main line on the edge of East Wichel housing development, which has an isolated cut and watered section, creating an attractive feature frontage to the development. Further stretches of new canal will probably be incorporated as a feature in the 'Eastern Villages Development', which will take the new main line from the south around the east of Swindon's main conurbation.

The East Wichel isolated section will be connected to the old main line south of a Waitrose store and is called 'The Wichelstowe Link'. On the canal side, there is a landing stage at Waitrose for boat trips on the restored section of the old main line of the canal.

The junction of the North Wilts Canal with the main line was near the Golden Lion Bridge, so called because the Golden Lion public house was situated close by. The bridge was demolished in 1918, four years after the canal was abandoned. The bridge crossed the Wilts & Berks Canal

The North Wilts arm of the Wilts & Berks Canal left the main line near Golden Lion Bridge, which was painted on the end of a terraced house in 1976 by Ken White and restored in 2009. (SU 153 849)

at the junction of Regent and Bridge streets, and is remembered on a mural painted on the end of a terraced house close to the site of the bridge.

East of Swindon and over the county boundary at Acorn Bridge, much work is necessary, but a new junction has been constructed near Culham Lock on the Thames for the Wilts & Berks to join the river, as the old junction site at Abingdon cannot be used. This amounts to 150 yards of canal with a winding hole. Ironically, none of the new canal will be in Berkshire following county boundary changes in 1976. Inevitably, the progress recorded here regarding the restoration of the Wilts & Berks Canal will become outdated as more finance is raised and permissions sought to move the project forward.

Above: The junction of the North Wilts with the Wilts & Berks *c*1890. Golden Lion Bridge is in the middle distance. (Courtesy of the Wilts and Swindon History Centre)

Right: The Swindon canal milestone indicating the distance to, and direction of, Semington. It is situated on Canal Walk in New Town on the site of the canal's main line. (SU 150 848)

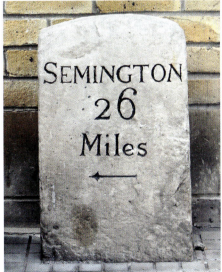

Chapter 8

The North Wilts Canal

T he North Wilts Canal was constructed to form a link between the Wilts & Berks Canal and the Thames and Severn Canal at Latton. An Act of Parliament was passed in 1813 allowing the construction of the canal under the name of the Severn Junction Canal, but it was later changed to the North Wilts Canal.

Work started in 1814. It left the main line of the Wilts & Berks in what was a rural location south of Swindon (old) town, currently where a department store is now situated in the town, and took a course north and to the east of the present-day railway junction to Gloucester.

The distance from the junction site at Swindon to Latton Basin is eight miles. The canal drops 60 feet through 12 locks. At Cricklade, a tunnel was necessary due to the lie of the land.

The North Wilts opened in 1819 but did not remain independent for long, as the Wilts & Berks purchased the company in 1820. Coal was the principal commodity carried on the canal in its early years. Movement was from the Staffordshire and Forest of Dean coalfields moving south and from the Somerset coalfield moving north. Other trade involved the movement of grain, timber, building materials and general merchandise.

Its most profitable years were in the early railway construction era of the late 1830s and early 1840s, when materials were carried to create its infrastructure. As with other Wiltshire canals, this proved to be the eventual downfall of the waterway.

The junction of the North Wilts Canal with the Wilts & Berks main line, *c*1910.

A pen and ink drawing of John Street Bridge in Swindon *c*1890. (Courtesy of Wilts and Swindon History Centre)

Purton Road Bridge, the present southern end of a restored section skirting Mouldon Country Park. (SU 121 873)

Above left: Looking north from Purton Road Bridge at the Mouldon Park section of restored canal. (SU 121 873)

Above right: Mouldon Lock restored but not in water as seen in 2017. (SU 119 873)

Below: Moredon Aqueduct over the river Ray showing restoration. (SU 114 878)

There is a short section of isolated canal in water at Hayes Knoll running adjacent to a country lane. (SU 104 907)

Further along the lane, towards Cricklade, the canal has been filled in. Seen in 2017. (SU 100 918)

Latton Basin seen from the information board viewpoint. The wall of the lock to enter the North Wilts Canal is in the top centre of the picture. Below this is the basin. In the foreground, when the canal was operational, there was an aqueduct to take the canal over the river and into the Thames and Severn Canal. (SU 083 956)

The entrance to Latton Basin from the Thames and Severn Canal, seen on the extreme left of the photograph (filled in) in 2018. (SU 083 956)

After the breach of Stanley Aqueduct in 1901, access from the south was restricted and it largely fell out of use. The last boat through the canal was in 1911 and then it slowly fell into dereliction and, like the Wilts & Berks, it was abandoned.

As with the Wilts & Berks main line, there is a desire to bring the North Wilts Canal back to life. There is also much to do, but some restoration has taken place and other work is in hand, depending upon accessibility and land ownership.

The Cricklade branch of the Wilts & Berks Canal Trust was formed in December 2000 and is responsible for the restoration of five miles of canal from Moredon Aqueduct to Latton Junction. The river Key aqueduct south of Cricklade has been restored and Hayes Knoll Lock was purchased in 2005.

The basin at Latton Junction and the old lock keeper's cottage still exist but is in private hands. The North Wilts Canal starts at the lock next to the basin. The basin was part of the Thames & Severn Canal, as is the junction, but for completeness of the remains, the start point begins from the junction with the Thames & Severn, particularly as the basin was used by both companies to transfer cargo between large masted vessels and smaller narrow boats. The North Wilts was a narrow canal, whereas the Thames & Severn was a wide waterway taking Thames barges and sailing trows, which were able to lower their masts to negotiate bridges.

The transfer of goods between barges and narrowboats was time consuming, so narrowboats began using the Thames & Severn Canal, despite some of the locks being only 68ft long and the narrowboats being 72ft long. To accommodate them, perhaps the narrowboats were corner to corner within the lock. The option for the narrowboats to use the Thames & Severn, thence down the North Wilts and Wilts & Berks to Abingdon, saved switching cargos at Latton and avoided the upper reaches of the Thames. Trade on the Latton to Lechlade section of the Thames and Severn dwindled in favour of the North Wilts.

At the Swindon end of the North Wilts, the junction has been built over. Further north is Mouldon Country Park with the North Wilts skirting its edge, the towpath seen as an amenity within the park. A section of the canal was restored. Unfortunately, it is overgrown now, but a rebuilt Mouldon Lock appears ready for gates.

Decades may pass before restoration of this northern arm of the Wilts & Berks will be completed.

Chapter 9

The Thames and Severn Canal in Wiltshire

The Thames and Severn Canal meanders briefly into Wiltshire after it leaves the Thames at Inglesham Lock. Inglesham is in Wiltshire, but the lock is across the Thames from the village and in Gloucestershire. Much like the Wilts & Berks Canal, it is under restoration. The path of the canal enters Wiltshire east of Marston Meysey and is presently filled in at this location. Here, there is a roundhouse, similar to that at Inglesham, once used by a lengthsman, but now a private residence. Originally the roof of the roundhouse was an inverted cone to collect the rainwater. A lengthsman was responsible for a defined length of towpath and canal, and his duties included the prevention of erosion on the canal banks, keeping vegetation down and the towpath clear and in a good state of repair. His duties would also include keeper of the lock if one or more existed on his patch.

Another roundhouse exists at Cerney Wick with a conventional cone roof. This is where the canal leaves Wiltshire and re-enters Gloucestershire. The lock here was partially restored in 1994. However, the old route of the canal in the vicinity of the A419 trunk road cannot be used and a detour has been proposed. Before Cerney Wick, the route of the canal passes Latton Basin, which was the junction with the North Wilts extension of the Wilts & Berks Canal, which is also planned to be restored. It is probable that the future restored North Wilts will join the Thames and Severn nearer Cricklade.

The Cotswolds Canal Trust aims to restore the whole length of the Thames and Severn Canal from its junction with the Stroudwater Navigation to the River Thames at Inglesham. The

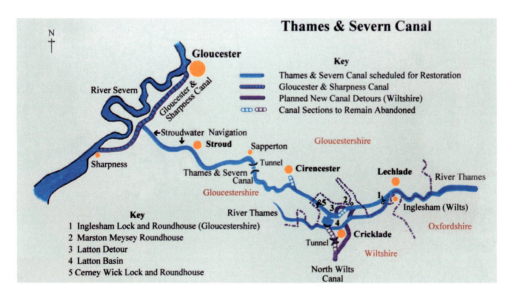

Thames & Severn Canal

Key
- ▬▬ Thames & Severn Canal scheduled for Restoration
- ▬▬ Gloucester & Sharpness Canal
- ▬▬ Planned New Canal Detours (Wiltshire)
- ⊂⊃⊂⊃ Canal Sections to Remain Abandoned

Key
1. Inglesham Lock and Roundhouse (Gloucestershire)
2. Marston Meysey Roundhouse
3. Latton Detour
4. Latton Basin
5. Cerney Wick Lock and Roundhouse

Inglesham Lock and roundhouse on the River Thames, near Lechlade. The Thames and Severn Canal starts immediately in front of the camera position, but is unfortunately obscured by the weeping willow. (SU 205 988)

Inglesham Lock and roundhouse, c1904.

restoration also includes the Stroudwater Navigation. The complete works will take many years to finish, as a major part of the route still requires substantial funding.

It is 36 miles from the Severn to the Thames via waterways. The Stroudwater Navigation was first mooted in 1730 and designed to create a through waterway from London to Bristol, with Acts of Parliament being passed in 1730 and 1776. There are 12 locks on the Stroudwater Navigation, which opened in 1779. The route is actively being restored under the first phase of restoration of the Thames and Severn project.

Marston Meysey roundhouse, *c*1910.

A further Act of Parliament was passed in 1783 covering the 28¾ miles of the Thames and Severn Canal between Stroud and Inglesham, to include 44 locks. There was also a 1½ mile branch to Cirencester planned. The most significant engineering feature of this canal is Sapperton Tunnel. It was designed as a broad tunnel 15ft wide and 15ft high in the centre. At 3,817 yards, it was the longest tunnel of any kind built in Britain at the time and was the last feature to be completed before the canal was opened in April 1789 but the last 3½ miles to Inglesham and the Thames did not open until near the end of that year.

The reason why this last section had not been completed was the navigable state of the upper Thames, which required dredging and the provision of new locks. Alternative routes were discussed, but in the final event the original route that had been given approval by the Act of Parliament was maintained. It was hoped the Thames Commissioners would fulfil their obligations to keep the Thames navigable on its upper reaches as far as Lechlade. The Thames and Severn Canal started a short distance upstream from the town. However, by the end of December 1789, the canal was open to its full length and the first cargo of coal from Staffordshire reached Lechlade. This lowered the cost of the coal to the local community, through more efficient transportation, by more than 30 per cent.

The Thames and Severn Canal closed through lack of traffic and eventual deterioration in 1933, with the Stroudwater Navigation following some years later. The canal frequently suffered from lack of water at the summit and this section was closed on a number of occasions. In 1875, the shortage of water resulted in only shallow-draught barges being allowed over the canal summit. In 1882, the GWR acquired the canal and, by this time, the railway linking Swindon with Gloucester had drastically reduced traffic on the waterway and played a significant role in the closure of the canal.

Nevertheless, between 1895 and 1900, there were attempts to keep the canal in operation. The last was when Gloucester County Council acquired the canal under a warrant of abandonment from the former proprietor. It spent much time and money trying to restore it to a viable waterway. The last officially recorded carriage of goods to Lechlade was a quantity of stone on 11 May 1911. Most of the staff east of Chalford to the Sapperton Tunnel and beyond to Inglesham had been dismissed in 1912. After this, the canal fell out of use and was officially closed in 1933.

Thames and Severn Canal mileposts. These are both at Eysey. (SU 113 944) They stand sentinel outside Eysey Manor Farm entrance and show the distances from Walbridge at the Stroudwater end of the canal and Inglesham at the Thames end. These stones register mileages that are a half mile apart, indicating one of them at least has been moved half a mile to join the other. When the distances to each end destination are added together, it shows the length of the canal to be 28¾ miles.

The Wiltshire section of the canal and the length between the county boundary to the Inglesham Thames Gateway Lock is being restored under phase 2 of the restoration programme. This phase covers the route from Gateway Bridge in the Cotswold Water Park at Cerney Wick through Wiltshire to Inglesham Lock, a distance of 10 miles. In 2002, British Waterways purchased the lock and associated roundhouse to safeguard access to the Severn and Thames canal waterway.

In 2009, the Cotswolds Canal Trust was given the freehold of Inglesham Lock. The Inland Waterways Association and the Waterways Recovery Group (WRG) have adopted the funding and restoration of the lock and work on the lock chamber was being undertaken by the WRG in 2016. The roundhouse adjacent to the canal has been purchased from British Waterways by a Canal Trust member.

The actions completed to date covering phase 2 are the construction of Gateway Bridge, the restoration of Eisey and Cerney Wick locks (structure only at this stage as the canal at these locations is not filled), towpath reconstructions, and dredging of the pound between Gateway Bridge and Cerney Wick Lock. However, perhaps the most important provision is the construction of a culvert under the A419 Latton bypass for the canal to pass under this trunk road. Because there was no immediate prospect of opening the canal at this location when the road was built, it was temporarily buried.

Weymoor bridge over the derelict canal at Latton has been restored and was complete in 2020. In 2024, the lock at Cerney Wick has little changed since my photograph, except the vista now has a romantic impression worthy of an artist's brush! Passing the canal under the A419 trunk road has not been attempted yet.

The lock and roundhouse are easily found from Lechlade Halfpenny Bridge – the roundhouse is signposted from the bridge and is a pleasant walk along the bank of the river.

There are five roundhouses situated on the canal, three in Gloucestershire, including Inglesham and two in Wiltshire; both are private residences. The Marston Maisey roundhouse is at present inaccessible, but that at Cerney Wick is situated next to the partially restored lock of the same name. The towpath is a public footpath in both directions from this location.

There is a broken example of a milestone close to Spine Road Bridge (Gateway Bridge, SU 072 972), between Cerney Wick and Wildmoorway Lower Lock. Both the lock and milestone are a stone's throw into Gloucestershire and I have included them for their feature interest.

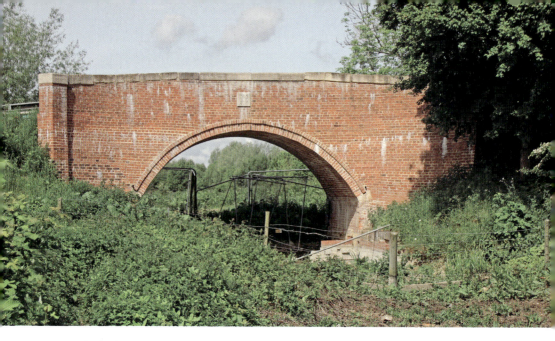

Above: Weymoor Bridge in Latton was completed and open to passage in 2020. It bears a stone date plaque of 2016, presumably when the main brickwork was completed. The bridge was built to carry farm carts over the canal to Latton Basin in *c*1788.

Left: The Thames and Severn Canal in water after very heavy rainfall during the winter of 2017/8. Photographed north-west of Latton Basin in March 2018. (SU 087 955)

I photographed the upstream end of Cerney Wick Lock in 1994. The photograph shows the wooden balance arm of the gate intact and apparently restored.

Above: The lock gates and cill of Cerney Wick Lock in September 2016. Note the balance arm has rotted and collapsed. (SU 079 961)

Right: Cerney Wick lock showing restored chamber in 2016. Adjacent is a roundhouse, now a private residence with no public access to that bank of the lock. The roundhouse, once a lengthman's house, together with the lock, are Grade II listed. Facing upstream on the canal leads to Spine Road (Gateway) Bridge and Wildmoorway Lock and keeper's cottage. Downstream from it is a signpost to Cricklade. Photographed in 2016. (SU 079 960)

Spine Road or Gateway Bridge is the boundary between Wiltshire and Gloucestershire and was rebuilt in 2004. (SU 072 972)

Left: The view along the towpath towards Cerney Wick Lock south of Spine Road Bridge. (SU 072 971)

Below: Wildmoorway Lower Lock seen from under the bridge, with the restored keeper's cottage above the bridge. This attractive feature is easily seen from Spine Road Bridge, and although in Gloucestershire is a short walk on the tow path. (SU 071 973)

RAILWAYS

Chapter 10

Wiltshire's Railways

Unlike canals, there is no path along the side of railways, except for the Berks and Hants line through the Kennet Valley, which has the Kennet and Avon Canal and its towpath running in close attention all the way from the county boundary at Froxfield to Savernake. After Savernake Tunnel, the canal flirts with the railway until the line approaches Pewsey, above which the Avon rises.

Other than this stretch in Wiltshire, we catch sight of the railway at stations, bridges, adjacent roadsides and with trains running through the Wiltshire landscape, typically in the Avon Valley beyond Bradford on Avon as far as the county boundary at Dundas Aqueduct.

In steam days, one could hear the huff and puff of locomotives working hard using mechanical horsepower, and see smoke and steam billowing into the sky. Today, the hum of an electric train leaves no evidence of its passing, but the landscape is scarred with catenary wires and regularly spaced metal masts on a growing number of railways in Wiltshire.

The railways of Wiltshire involved two major competitors; the Great Western Railway (GWR) and the London & South Western Railway (L&SWR). The GWR's lines were primarily in the centre and north of the county and the L&SWR in the south. Other players built railway lines crossing the county north to south and others still built branch lines, mostly with the support of the two main rivals. Sometimes the rivalry was intense.

In 1923, the Great Western Railway and the Southern Railway were the rail operating organisations in Wiltshire, other than a small number of private and military railways. At nationalisation of the rail network in 1948, the Southern Railway became the Southern Region of British Railways and the Great Western became the Western Region.

5904 *Kelham Hall* speeds past Little Bedwyn church with a stopping train, probably to Trowbridge on 25 June 1959. The Kennet and Avon Canal runs parallel at this point and is in weed-free condition despite being out of use to through traffic for a number of years.

Signs of electrification are evident at Tockenham with masts being placed trackside on 7 September 2016. The HST 125 unit is headed by power car 43127 on its way from Bristol to Paddington. Most of these HST sets have become surplus to requirements as lines are electrified. However, some of the sets were refurbished into two-power cars and four-coach trains, known as Castle sets, being named after castles in the region. These were operating between Penzance and Cardiff, but during 2023 some of these were withdrawn, leaving just four of the sets in operation during 2024.

The mess of privatisation followed decades later, offering one distinct advantage for the railway enthusiast and perhaps, even for passengers: liveries of the different operating companies add colour and variety to the trains. The freight trains operating through Wiltshire have different owner engines at the helm.

The Great Western was renowned for building short terminal branch lines to reach small towns that the main line railways had bypassed for reasons of geology, gradient or merely to keep the route from one centre to another as short as possible. Branch lines existed to a lesser extent on the L&SWR, at least until Devon and Cornwall were reached.

Warship D823 *Hermes* at Salisbury with an Exeter train in 1969. *Hermes* was built at Swindon in 1960 and was withdrawn from service in 1972. It is said that the Swindon-built Warships (D800–832 and D866–870) were most frequently seen on the Exeter services.

In Wiltshire, there were GWR terminal branch lines to Calne, Highworth, Malmesbury, Marlborough and Tidworth (M&SWJR). The L&SWR built a branch to Amesbury, although it was originally intended to reach Shrewton. There were a number of branch lines built that were low on traffic until needed as diversionary routes.

There were two broadly north to south routes through the county: The Midland & South Western Junction Railway was absorbed by the GWR at the grouping in 1923 and ran through Wiltshire from Cricklade to Ludgershall, originating in Cheltenham and ending at Andover Junction. The whole line closed to passengers in 1961, but isolated stubs remained for freight until 1970.

The Wilts, Somerset & Weymouth Railway ran from Thingley Junction, near Chippenham, through Westbury to Frome, with Weymouth as its destination. A branch to Devizes was included, which later connected with the Berks and Hants at Patney and Chirton. Extensions were built to Salisbury from Westbury and from Trowbridge to Bathampton. These routes are still open, with exception of the Devizes line, albeit the original route between Thingley Junction and Trowbridge now has only a sparse service. The line between Bathampton and Salisbury is presently well used and forms the Wessex main line.

During World War One, the Salisbury Plain area became a training and camping ground for thousands of troops, many of them from New Zealand and Australia. The camps needed supplies, so short-lived branch lines sprang up from the existing through railways – these were classified as military railways and often had their own motive power.

Class 33 no. 33027 *Earl Mountbatten of Burma* seen near Avoncliff on the Wessex main line on 14 May 1988.

It is ironic that despite regionalisation in 1948, privatisation and various company names in the intervening years, the old GWR is still the GWR for its passenger services. The old L&SWR is now the South Western Railway, only London is missing from the title.

So, what will happen to Wiltshire's railways in the future? The South Wales main line has been electrified, but progress is slow to Bristol and the West. New 800 Class IET (Intercity Express Trains) have been introduced, which are capable of running electrically on overhead wires or by diesel power. The L&SWR route to Exeter is still a poor relation to the Berks and Hants route to the West Country, but has been improved with reintroduction of double track in places to improve capacity.

New stations have been proposed in Wiltshire, replacing those lost in the Beeching cuts of the 1960s. When and if the following will be built will depend upon finance and the will to reduce road traffic in the respective places – Royal Wootton Bassett, Corsham, Devizes Parkway, Porton and Stonehenge and Wilton Junction (previously proposed as Wilton Parkway). Until the new stations are built and officially opened none of the names seem to be finalised.

Chapter 11

The Great Western Main Line

The Great Western Railway was founded in 1833 and was enabled by an Act of Parliament in 1835, with Isambard Kingdom Brunel as its engineer. In 1838, Brunel opened the first stage of the Great Western Railway between Paddington and Bristol as far as Maidenhead on the eastern bank of the Thames. After completing the magnificent Sounding Arch bridge, progress was rapid and Swindon was reached by November 1840. A temporary terminus was built at Wootton Bassett Road, west of Swindon, which opened on 17 December 1840.

At the Bristol end of the line, construction commenced on a terminus in 1839 and by the end of August 1840 train services were operating to Bath. There remained one major obstruction to completing the line – Box Hill and the tunnel beneath it, which was proposed in the original Act of Parliament authorising the line.

The strata of Box Hill required assessment prior to construction work. It was known that the geology of the hill was mainly composed of great oolite limestone, known as Bath stone in the locality, and inferior oolite limestone. In 1836 and '37, Brunel sank eight shafts along the railway's proposed alignment to determine the ease or difficulty of working through the hill's rock.

The construction of the tunnel commenced from both ends simultaneously. From the western portal, the company contracted was George Burge of Herne Bay, which was to construct seven per cent of the tunnel work. From the east, local contractor, Lewis and Brewer, shared the remainder. Work on the tunnel commenced in December 1838.

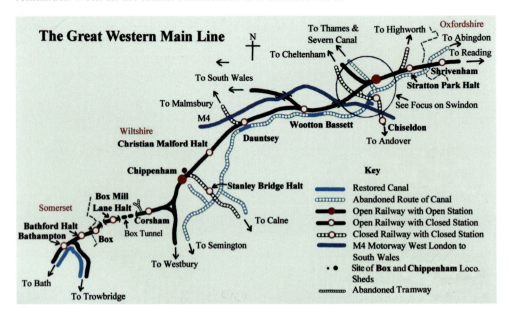

A major factor in achieving the correct alignment from east to west was the construction of ventilation shafts, which were all 25 feet in diameter, but ranged from 70ft deep at the east end to more than 290ft deep at the western end. Through these shafts went all the movement of spoil as well as the tunnel access for the workers, which was achieved with the aid of steam-powered winches. The only available light was candlelight.

Labour was cheap and expendable; time was of the essence. Blasting using explosives was conducted with men inside the tunnels. Explosions often released torrents of water, both being factors in the high loss of life of the navvies engaged in the construction work (approaching 100). The ingress of water proved to be a major problem and additional pumping arrangements had to be put in place, causing delays in completion of the tunnel. When the two ends of the tunnel were joined in April 1841 there was less than two inches of misalignment.

The tunnel opened to traffic with a through route established between Paddington and Bristol on 30 June 1841. The portal at the Box village end of the tunnel, designed by Brunel in a classical style, was incomplete at its opening.

The main line was originally built in broad gauge at 7ft ¼in, but from 1861, standard 4ft 8½in gauge was added to create dual gauge from Paddington, reaching Swindon by 1872 and Bath by 1875. Broad gauge was removed throughout the Great Western network in 1892, leaving the principal network of the United Kingdom as standard gauge.

The western portal of the 3,212yd-long Box tunnel seen with a Star Class 4-6-0, emerging with an express train to Bristol, c1925. Note the empty low-sided stone wagons in the siding, the engine stop board and the height of the tunnel bore. Here the line's gradient is rising at 1 in 100 towards Swindon.

The stations built in Wiltshire upon opening or shortly after were, from east to west, Swindon, Wootton Bassett, Dauntsey, Chippenham, Corsham and Box. The station and railway environment in and around Swindon is dealt with in greater detail in the chapter 'Focus on Swindon'.

Subsequent to the principal stations, three halts were built in the 20th century, one of which was at Stratton Park. Some sources suggest that it was opened with the line in 1840 and others that it was opened in 1933. It is probable that it opened as a halt in 1933, when the outskirts of Swindon were expanding. A 1910 working timetable does not list it. Another halt was opened at Christian Malford near Chippenham in 1926 and one at Box Mill Lane in 1930.

The GWR main line from Paddington enters the county of Wiltshire shortly after leaving Shrivenham. Here the Wilts & Berks Canal had to be bridged to allow it to pass under the railway on its way from Semington to Abingdon.

I have memories of travelling on local stopping trains from Didcot to Swindon and remember the train stopping at Stratton Park Halt, a very simple affair with two short platforms and a corrugated waiting shelter on each one. Stratton Park, from the railway line, appeared rural back in 1958, but the view through the carriage window changed dramatically once the train passed under the road bridge adjacent to the station. Sidings and industrial units started to appear in growing profusion.

I will leave Swindon at this point and skip west to Royal Wootton Bassett. A few miles before the site of Wootton Bassett station was Wootton Bassett Road. This was the site of a temporary terminus in 1840 of the GWR main line from Paddington. The station in the small town of Wootton Bassett opened in 1841 and Wootton Bassett Road closed.

The station was rebuilt for the opening of the South Wales direct line in 1903 and its name changed to Wootton Bassett Junction. The station and goods facilities were closed in 1965 as

The Cheltenham Spa Express seen near Stratton Park Halt in 1962, hauled by Castle Class no. 7000 *Viscount Portal*.

part of the Beeching axe, but there remains a Foster Yeoman stone siding served by stone trains from the Mendip Yeoman quarry.

A near-fatal accident occurred on 7 March 2015 when a steam excursion hauled by Battle of Britain 34067 *Tangmere* passed a signal at Danger (SPAD). The charter excursion applied brakes, but failed to stop before the junction with the South Wales line and straddled the junction. Just 44 seconds prior to this, an HST had passed at speed.

Class 66 no. 66502 *Basford Hall Centenary 2001* leaves Wootton Bassett with a Wentloog to Southampton Freightliner on 07 September 2016. (SU 075 817)

Wootton Bassett station yard populated with horses and carts, illustrating the mode of goods transport, *c*1908.

A Cornish express passes under Cocklebury Bridge in 1909.

In 1955, a Bristol-bound express enters Chippenham with Castle Class no. 5010 *Restormal Castle* in charge.

Dauntsey station was opened in 1868 and was situated, not in Dauntsey village, but a few miles south near Dauntsey Lock on the Wilts and Berks Canal. The station was the junction for the Malmesbury branch from 1877 (*see* Malmesbury Railway). Subsequent to the opening of the South Wales Direct Railway, the branch line started from Little Somerford and Dauntsey lost its junction for Malmesbury status. The station remained open until 1965, but the canopy over the branch platform was removed to Yatton station in Somerset and remains there to this day.

Chippenham station in 1955.

Between Dauntsey and Chippenham lies the village of Christian Malford, which received a halt in 1926. Eight down trains and nine up stopped there on weekdays in 1947; a good service, basically running between Swindon and Chippenham, with some trains extended to Bristol.

Chippenham station opened on 31 May 1841 and was expanded in 1858 with a locomotive and goods sheds. There is evidence of Brunel's involvement in the construction of the line with his offices still extant in the station yard. This building, along with the Western Arches viaduct, a short distance to the west, are part of Chippenham Civic Society's Blue Plaque Trail. The station is constructed out of local ashlar Bath stone and is Grade II listed.

The station was the junction for the Calne branch. The locomotive shed was situated slightly east of the station on the up side and in 1947 housed 0-6-0 no 3215; 0-6-0PT (Pannier Tanks) nos 3684, 3748, 4651, 8779, 9720 and 9721; 0-4-2T nos 1433, 1453. The latter were employed on Calne branch trains.

The locomotive shed closed in 1964 with the loss of pick-up goods traffic and the demise of steam generally on the Western Region. Traffic on the Calne branch ended in 1965.

Modifications to the track layout took place in 1976 and the down platform was taken out of use. Diesel-hydraulic Hymeks were used for the engineering trains involved. From the commencement of services after the layout changes, all trains used the island platform faces and do so to this day.

The footpath footbridge at the Bath end of the station was demolished in 2016 and rebuilt with ticket barrier access to the platforms in readiness for electrification. By 2023, powered electrification had reached Langley Burrell, but the spiraling cost has left the future of the full route's electrification in doubt.

Above: The offices used by Brunel in the construction of the GWR main line through Chippenham and the commemorative blue plaque attached to the wall. (ST 918 736)

Left: The Western Arches, built in 1841 and widened in 1848. (ST 921 737)

Above: Chippenham had its own locomotive shed, which was classed as a sub-depot to the home shed at Swindon, coded SDN in GWR days and 82C following nationalisation in 1948. Here, 5700 pannier tank no. 4606 rests between duties on 23 September 1956.

Right: Reorganisation of the track layout at Chippenham in 1976, when the down main platform was taken out of use.

West of Chippenham is Thingley sidings on the north side of the line opposite Thingley Junction, which is presently single track and used for Westbury-bound trains on what is often referred to as the Wessex Line (See Wilts, Somerset & Weymouth Railway). The sidings at Thingley and the large train shed were built in 1937 for military use. More recently they have seen little use, perhaps on occasion for departmental trains.

Corsham station, situated about a mile east of Box Tunnel, was in a cutting, resulting in the main station building being sited at the top of the cutting on the town side of the railway. There were a number of sidings west of the station, with a goods shed and loading dock. The principal traffic in the goods yard was quarried stone from the quarry under Box Hill.

The down main platform with rails removed. On the down side of the island platform, a Bristol service with HST power cars 43053 (leading) and 43030 has made a scheduled stop.

A 2ft 5½in tramway brought the stone to the station yard. The tramway system was authorised by the Board of Trade in 1876 and eventually involved five branch lines. In addition, a private standard-gauge line ran alongside the main line to access the stone under Box Hill via an adjacent tunnel to the main bore of the GWR. This siding was connected to the GWR near the station and was probably built *c*1865, though was out of use by *c*1950. Originally, it may have been broad gauge and converted sometime between 1874 and 1892.

The station closed in 1965, with general goods traffic from the yard ceasing two years earlier, but the loading dock siding remained in situ until 1978. Moves were afoot in 2017 to attempt the reopening of a station at Corsham, which could see a new through train service between Bristol and Oxford, but it is highly unlikely that any Bristol to Paddington trains would ever stop there in the foreseeable future. Work on the rebuilding of Corsham station is planned to start in 2026 and for the station to be operational in 2028.

Corsham station and goods yard, *c*1910.

Above: The station sidings full of stone wagons, *c*1905.

Right: Castle Class no. 7017 *G.J. Churchward* at Corsham station in 1961.

Opposite: The tail end of an HST on a Paddington-bound service is about to enter the western portal of Box Tunnel on 9 June 2016.

Right: The scene from the top of Middle Hill Tunnel, with King Class no. 6024 *King Edward I* on the down road with the John Betjeman Special in October 2014.

Below: Box Mill Lane Halt on 25 September 1960.

The main Bath Road (A4) crosses the cutting in front of the western portal of Box Tunnel. On the north side of the line there were some sidings for stone traffic, which have long been dismantled, leaving no evidence of their existence.

Between Box Tunnel and the much shorter Middle Hill Tunnel was Box Mill Lane Halt. It was opened in 1930 and presumably thought necessary because it was closer to the village centre than Box station, which was on the western outskirts.

There is an excellent view of the line out of Box Tunnel and under the A4 from an accessible parapet on the top of Middle Hill Tunnel. Box station was situated to the west of Middle Hill Tunnel. It was built for the opening of the line in 1841, rebuilt around 1855 and the platforms probably extended at the same time.

Of interest was the employment of a banking engine for heavy goods trains climbing the 1 in 100 rising gradient through the tunnel. A purpose-built shed was erected near the station (closed in 1919). The locomotive was rehoused in Chippenham shed, but with the advent of more powerful and efficient locomotives, banking duties would probably have been few and far between.

On the north side of the line, the station yard was used for stone traffic and general goods.

The line crosses into Somerset shortly after Box, passing the closed station site of Bathford Halt, before the Wessex line comes in from Westbury.

Left: **Box station and yard, *c*1905. The shed in the left foreground may have been where the banking engine was housed as there are steam/smoke vents in the roof.**

Below: **46233, running in LMS livery as 6233 *Duchess of Sutherland*, approaches Box with a return Victoria to Exeter excursion on 30 April 2022.**

Chapter 12

Focus on Swindon Junction and Railway Works

Swindon is a little over 77 miles from Paddington on Brunel's Great Western Railway main line to Bristol. Railway construction had reached Challow, then called Farringdon Road, on 20 July 1840. Progress was rapid and by 17 December, the line had progressed through Swindon to a point a short distance from Wootton Bassett at Hay Lane. At this juncture there was

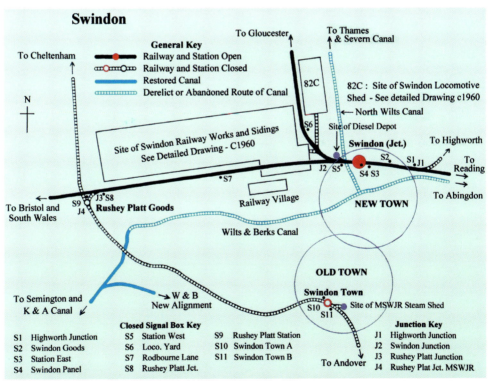

The map of Swindon shows the location of signal boxes from 1912 to the opening of the Panel Box in 1968 (now closed), with signalling controlled from Didcot since 2016. Prior to 1909, Swindon's boxes were lettered A to F, with Highworth Junction being 'A' and Rodbourne Lane 'F'. Swindon 'E' (Gloucester Junction) closed in 1909. It also shows the route of the North Wilts and Wilts & Berks Canals, which played a vital role in transporting coal to fire the engines of the infant Great Western Railway in the 1840s. The Wagon Works and associated buildings to the right of the locomotive depot are not shown for clarity.

no station built at Swindon. However, upon the decision to build the GWR locomotive works on a green field site below the small town of Swindon, the situation was remedied in 1842.

The Cheltenham & Great Western Union Railway had opened a line as far as Cirencester from Swindon in May 1841, continuing to Cheltenham via Gloucester by 1845, eventually joining up with South Wales Railways and reaching Swansea in 1852. The junction at Swindon to Gloucester from the Bristol main line became the South Wales main line, long before the Severn Tunnel was constructed.

Until 1895, every train stopped at Swindon Junction station for 10 minutes to change locomotives and for passengers to refresh themselves on the four-hour journey between Paddington and Bristol. Refreshment rooms were built at the station under an agreement with contractors, the first such facility at any station in Britain.

The station was built of three storeys. The refreshment rooms were easily accessible from the trains to minimise delays. Queen Victoria was reputed to have used the refreshment rooms. The higher floors comprised the station hotel and lounge. By the 1890s, journey times had shortened and it became inconvenient to hold trains at Swindon.

The original building on the down side was demolished in 1972 to make way for a modern station entrance with office facilities above.

The siting of a railway shed and workshops were beneficial for the change in engines required before the steeper graded line between Swindon and Bristol was undertaken. Locomotives with smaller-diameter driving wheels were necessary, rather than the 7ft wheels used on the relatively flat track between Paddington and Swindon. Furthermore, Swindon was to become an important junction of railways and it would be necessary to service locomotives used on the Gloucester and Swindon Junction Railway.

Significant too was the presence of canals in Swindon, with routes closely associated with both the Bristol line and north, following the railway to Gloucester. The latter, the North Wilts

2200 Class no. 2244 works hard on a freight through Swindon on 4 February 1963.

Canal, allowed connection to the Thames & Severn Canal, which in turn connected with the Bristol Channel and the South Wales coalfield. Another option connected the Somerset coalfield with the Wilts & Berks Canal, via The Somerset Coal Canal and the Kennet & Avon. Ironically, the canals initially helped service the Great Western Railway with coal, but as the railways expanded in the remaining part of the 19th century, they spelt doom for the less efficient waterways.

On 6 October 1840, the directors of the GWR approved Swindon as the site for its railway workshops and engine shed. The labour required to successfully operate the establishment needed living accommodation. The small town of Swindon did not have the requisite workforce

Castle Class no. 5006 *Tregenna Castle* with the 11.55 Paddington to Milford Haven passing through Swindon station in August 1955.

2800 Class no 3819 runs through the centre line in Swindon with a freight in 1957.

Swindon station from the west taken in the early 1960s.

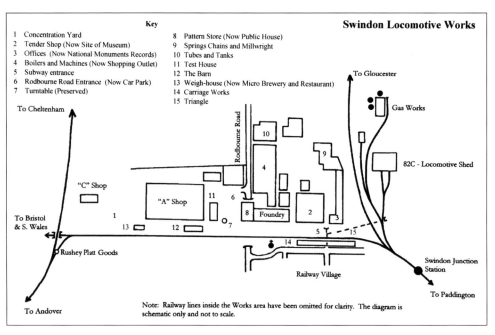

Key

Swindon Locomotive Works

1 Concentration Yard
2 Tender Shop (Now Site of Museum)
3 Offices (Now National Monuments Records)
4 Boilers and Machines (Now Shopping Outlet)
5 Subway entrance
6 Rodbourne Road Entrance (Now Car Park)
7 Turntable (Preserved)

8 Pattern Store (Now Public House)
9 Springs Chains and Millwright
10 Tubes and Tanks
11 Test House
12 The Barn
13 Weigh-house (Now Micro Brewery and Restaurant)
14 Carriage Works
15 Triangle

Note: Railway lines inside the Works area have been omitted for clarity. The diagram is schematic only and not to scale.

and the sudden demand for drafted-in skilled labour resulted in the construction of railway cottages just south of the Bristol main line and close to the workshops. This was known as the Railway Village, eventually consisting of 300 cottages. Each had a small front garden and a rear yard with washhouse and privy. An alley separated the rows of cottages, with access to the back yards.

A works building wall near the Steam Museum of Swindon entrance, using stone from the Box Tunnel area and showing the unusual feature of inverted arches. These reduce sideways force on the wall, but other forces have come into play over time and support has been provided to stop the wall from swelling. (SU 149 849)

The site of railway workshops to erect and repair locomotives and a principal engine shed to service them was an important consideration for Brunel and his Locomotive Superintendent, Daniel Gooch. It made sense to locate workshops on the route between Paddington and Bristol, rather than at each end of the line, where urban development had made land scarce and expensive. As the railway progressed west, both Reading and Didcot had been considered for a works facility, but it was a green field site below the small hill town of Swindon that was eventually selected.

Construction of the Railway Works started in 1841, using stone extracted from the bore of Box Tunnel. The facility became operational in 1843, with repairs to the various designs of locomotives from contractors and carrying out servicing of locomotives in an engine shed between the engineering section and the main running line to Bristol.

Initially the works operated as a repair shop only and did not manufacture its own Great Western engines, but variations in quality and non-standard components soon changed thinking. It became clear to Brunel and Gooch that locomotives designed and built at Swindon would reduce cost and many components could be standardised.

The first wholly built Swindon locomotive was initially named *Premier* for obvious reasons, but it was soon renamed *Great Western*. The broad-gauge single-wheeler was commissioned in

Above left and above right: **Part of the railway village, showing Exeter Street and its front gardens and a typical alley at the rear of the properties in 1981.**

The first locomotive to run on the GWR was the 1837 2-2-2 Charles Tayleur locomotive *Vulcan*. It was built at the Vulcan Foundry and was withdrawn in 1843. Presumably rapid improvement in design and reliability in those pioneering years rendered it outmoded. However, it was rebuilt as a 2-2-2 tank locomotive in 1846 and survived in this form until 1868. This depiction of the locomotive is on a tiled underpass wall leading to New Town shopping centre in Swindon. (SU 148 850)

Looking east over the broad-gauge locomotive dump sidings in 1892, on the future site of 'A' Shop, the main erecting shop, at Swindon Works. (Courtesy of Steam Museum of the GWR)

1846. Four years later, goods wagons began to be manufactured at the works and by 1867 the engineering facility became the principal workshop for carriages.

It was inevitable that sooner or later broad gauge would be converted to standard gauge, given that GWR stood alone with its wide-track system. In the 1870s, many lines had been dual gauge, enabling through trains to operate over Great Western metals north to south. By 1890, it became clear that a massive gauge conversion, in short time, to minimise disruption, would soon be necessary. Broad gauge was abolished commencing 20 May 1892.

Locomotives and rolling stock were moved to broad-gauge storage sidings at the western end of Swindon Works. Some were converted to standard gauge, but where conversion wasn't possible, stock was dismantled and scrapped.

A new erecting factory was constructed and completed in 1903 on the site of the broad-gauge storage sidings and named A Shop. The covered engineering space was 5¾ acres, large enough for two parallel streets of Swindon's railway village to be accommodated inside. In 1919, the space was doubled, making it the largest erecting shop in Britain.

Many iconic Great Western locomotives were manufactured in A Shop and towards the last years of steam traction, the works built some standard designs introduced from 1951.

The heyday of Swindon was in the 1920s and '30s when the Castle and King Class locomotives were introduced. There followed Halls and Granges, developments of earlier Saints. At the time, there was no hint of steam being phased out in favour of diesel and electric.

Right: Inside A Shop, *c*1958 with 6994 *Baggrave Hall* and 6015 *King Richard III* being overhauled. Entering the main shop right and left were seen long rows of locomotives in various states of undress.

Below: With paint drying in the sun, Modified Hall no. 7902 *Eaton Mascot Hall* stands ex works outside A Shop, *c*1958.

In 1958, the Western Region invested in a modernisation programme to introduce diesel-hydraulic motive power. The Class 41 Warships were introduced in 1958, as were the more numerous Class 42 Warships, with D800 *Sir Brian Robertson* being the first Swindon-built locomotive. The subsequent building programme was shared between Swindon and the North British Locomotive Company. In 1961, Class 35 Hymeks were introduced, but all were built by Beyer Peacock. In the same year came the Westerns, with the building programme being shared between Swindon and Crewe.

The final production run of diesel-hydraulic locomotives started in 1964 with 56 Class 14 centre-cab trip working locomotives. Unfortunately, pick-up goods from station goods yards started to be phased out soon after the Class 14 locomotives had been manufactured. They saw little service and were sold to private business, exported or scrapped. Many have since found their way into preservation and are useful additions to preserved railway fleets of locomotives.

Steam locomotives were still being repaired at Swindon in 1964, but only a few GWR-designed classes, typically Modified Halls and Granges. In May of that year, I was surprised to find a number of Ivatt Class 4 2-6-0s being repaired, including 43044 receiving attention in

Above: LNER V2 60922 /41 and 45 lined up in the Concentration Yard awaiting cutting up in C Shop in October 1964.

Left: In 1964, the works was repairing diesel shunters, which became the mainstay of its workload after the demise of hydraulics. In 1979, 08502 and 08021 were inside A Shop.

A Shop. Another visit in October recorded the strange sight of LNER V2 locomotives lined up in the scrap lines of the Concentration Yard waiting to be cut up.

The Western Region's decision to run hydraulics spelled the death knell for Swindon's iconic century-and-a-half railway adventure.

Inside C Shop, Mogul no. 5314 was being cut up in 1957.

In May 1964, Class 14s were under construction in the works. This photograph shows D9503 and 5904.

Castle Class no. 5017 *The Gloucestershire Regiment 28th 61st* by the works turntable, *c*1958.

Hall Class no. 5987 *Brocket Hall* outside 'The Barn' in ex-works condition, *c*1958.

The lines of withdrawn steam locomotives in the Concentration Yard awaiting cutting up during the 1960s were being replicated in the 1970s with short-lived diesel-hydraulic classes. Rows of Hymeks with little more than 10 years' service and Warships with similar life spans cluttered up sidings. In 1973, the Westerns were still operating, but by 1975 the yard at the western end of the Works held rows of faded paintwork and rusty locomotives that once were the pride of the modernised Western Region.

The lifespan of diesel hydraulics was relatively short compared to that of Great Western steam locomotives. The 1970s saw the mass withdrawal of Western Class locomotives. On 9 January 1977, a large number were awaiting scrapping. In the left row are 1063 *Western Monitor*, 1021 *Western Cavalier*, 1034 *Western Trooper*, 1011 *Western Thunderer*, 1005 *Western Venturer*, 1053 *Western Patriarch* and 1056 *Western Sultan*. On the right are: 1001 *Western Pathfinder*, 1054 *Western Governor*, and 1015 *Western Champion*. In all, there were 24 members of the class in the yard on that day, with others in other parts of the Works complex.

The first Class 46 to be cut up at Swindon Works was 46012. It was withdrawn in July 1980 and met its end in October of the same year.

As well as scrapping locomotives, the Works' main occupation during this period was the repair of diesel shunters and multiple units. By 1977, other classes of outdated and probably worn-out diesel electrics were being cut up at Swindon. The scrapping of Class 24 engines, for example, was shared between Swindon and Doncaster.

By 1980, A Shop was involved with the refurbishment of four-car 4-BEP Southern Region stock. Diesel shunters were still being repaired, but an increasing number were being dismantled for spares and many cabs were scattered around the yard, some being purchased privately as garden sheds. In the early years of the '80s, Swindon started scrapping more diesel-electric classes, mainly Class 20, 25, 40, 45 and 46.

A cosmetically restored Warship D818 *Glory* on 6 June 1981.

During the late 1970s, the Works held a series of open days, where steam made a brief return appearance as exhibits. A Grand Exhibition of Steam and the History of the Works was scheduled to take place in 1985, but an announcement that the Works was to close caused industrial unrest and the exhibition was cancelled. The Works finally closed in 1986.

In the 1840s, it was essential for a shed facility to service a locomotive at the end of its journeys, or exchange it for a freshly coaled and watered example.

The first loco shed for broad-gauge locomotives was situated adjacent to the Bristol main line, with the repair workshops constructed to its rear. The shed facilities were vastly improved in 1871 when a new shed was opened adjacent to the South Wales main line (via Gloucester). Initially this was a nine-road shed leading into a roundhouse at the rear. In 1908, the shed was enlarged to include a new roundhouse building, offices and stores. To the side and rear of the main shed building was a six-road stock shed, where spare locomotives were held in reserve. It was here that 4003 *Lode Star* and Dean Goods 2516 were kept pending restoration for museum exhibition.

The GWR used a letter code system to identify its engine sheds; Swindon was SDN. Post-nationalisation, British Railways adopted the LMS mode of shed identification and to that end a cast oval plate was placed near the base of the smokebox door. Swindon was in the Bristol Division and coded 82C. Various locomotives were out stationed at Andover Junction, Chippenham, Faringdon and Malmesbury. In 1947, there were 120 locomotives allocated, including those at sub-sheds. With the rapid run down of Western Region steam in the early '60s, it was too large and unsuitable to service diesel locomotives and closed along with its stock shed in 1964. Most of the remaining locomotives not withdrawn were transferred to Didcot and Gloucester.

A diminutive diesel shed later replaced the large steam shed facilities, which were situated on the north side of the line near the junction to Gloucester. The shed could be seen from a car park near the station on the south side of the track. The depot no longer exists and was probably dismantled at a similar time to that at Westbury, after 1990.

Electrification with overhead wires had reached Swindon in 2018, but moving west beyond Swindon saw slow progress. The principal services through Swindon are regular interval trains

2-6-2 Tank 8104 in front of Swindon shed on 15 October 1951.

57xx Class Pannier Tank no. 3677 in the roundhouse in 1964.

Dukedog 3212 *Earl of Eldon* in the shed yard at Swindon in 1936. Its name was removed in 1937 and given to Castle 5055.

The diminutive replacement loco shed at Swindon was hard pressed to service Standard Class 4 nos. 75069 and Jubilee 5690 *Leander* on 28 June 1986 with a Welsh Marches special.

to Paddington, South Wales, Bristol, Cheltenham and a stopping service to Westbury via Trowbridge. Freight consists of Somerset quarry workings, fuel tanks to Theale, Freightliners to South Wales and various other flows.

The express trains through Swindon were operated by diesel-hydraulic locomotives and Class 47 diesel-electrics after steam on the Western Region ceased at the end of 1965. In 1975, the first Class 253 HST125 units were introduced, entering service in 1976. Eventually these units took over all principal express services and continued to do so until the Class 800 electro-diesels were introduced in October 2017. These Hitachi units have slowly taken over from the HST 125 units on all Great Western electrified main lines.

There is an aftermath, perhaps more of a legacy, to the closure of Swindon Works in 1986. There has been much development of the massive site, and during this process many exhibits

Class 31 no. 31123 leaves Swindon with a parcels working on 3 August 1978.

of the past are retained to remind visitors of the previous importance of Swindon Railway Works and its role as a major employer in a conurbation that started as a minor town on a small hill in Wiltshire.

The Swindon Works turntable has been preserved on its original site, the weigh-house is part of a microbrewery, the pattern store is a public house and the original offices are now used for National Monuments Record. However, the two most important preserved building features – for the public – are the Swindon Outlet Shopping Centre and the Steam Museum.

The outlet centre was once the boiler makers' shop and associated machine tool areas and later in the 1970s dealt with wagons. Throughout the malls are exhibits reminding shoppers of the building's history. The factory department war memorials are also preserved on the building's walls.

The steam locomotive turntable is preserved near the Rodbourne Road car park. (SU 141 847)

Above: Churchward House, the old GWR drawing office, with a preserved traverser allowing wagons, for example, to be transferred to parallel tracks. (SU 143 850)

Left: In the Steam Museum a carpenter works on carriage construction. (With permission of Steam Museum)

The Steam Museum contains in its building fabric the original 1846 Machine and Fitting Shop. The main body of the building is the Machine and Turning Shop, which latterly served as a Wheel Shop. This museum houses a number of steam locomotives from the heyday of Swindon Locomotive Works and will, hopefully, give future generations an interest in Wiltshire railway eras of the 19th and 20th centuries.

Chapter 13

The Highworth Light Railway

Duting the rush to build railways, the community of Highworth was hopeful that it would find itself on a successful proposed route of the Great Western main line to Bristol. Unfortunately, the chosen route, through Swindon, was five miles south of the town. Swindon, in 1840, was little more than a small country hill town.

In 1873, interested parties in the town proposed that a branch line be built from Highworth to join the GWR main line to Bristol at a point below Stratton St Margaret. The railway was to be known as The Highworth Light Railway.

Above: **Stratton station remains after closure, *c*1968.**

Right: **Hannington station on 23 September 1956.**

Pannier no.1658 with a Gloucestershire Railway Society special at Hannington on 31 March 1962.

On 21 June 1875, an Act of Parliament was passed, giving the line approval to proceed with a share value of £28,000. Bad weather delayed the start until 1879. In reality, it was almost certainly finance, namely the difficulty of selling shares, that delayed the start, despite the initial enthusiasm. It took three years to raise enough capital and to find a suitable contractor. The shares were never completely sold and, as part payment for building the line, the chosen contractor agreed to accept £8,500 worth of shares in part payment.

There was always a trend to underestimate the cost of construction of the branch lines built in the early years of railways. For the completion of the Highworth branch, a further £8,000 was requested by the contractor.

The line was inspected in March 1881, but there were numerous faults to be rectified. The Highworth Light Railway had no further funds and, in effect, was bankrupt. Since the railway was joining the GWR main line, it was logical to offer the sale of the line to the GWR. On 7 June 1882, the GWR took over the assets of the Highworth Light Railway and it became a branch line of the parent company.

The GWR spent considerably more than the projected £8,000 to complete the railway to an approved standard. The line opened on 9 May to paying passengers. There were three intermediate stations; Stratton, Stanton and Hannington. It was never successful as a passenger line, but many factories were built, mostly in the vicinity of Stratton St. Margaret. It was very busy during the years of the two world wars, with the Brunner Mond munitions factory providing much traffic. Further freight movement was generated by Vickers Armstrong and a spur was built to serve the factory.

Goods fared better and Highworth did not close completely until 1962. During this time, an unadvertised workmen's train ran for Swindon Railway Works employees. A small vestige of the branch line has been retained at the junction end of the line.

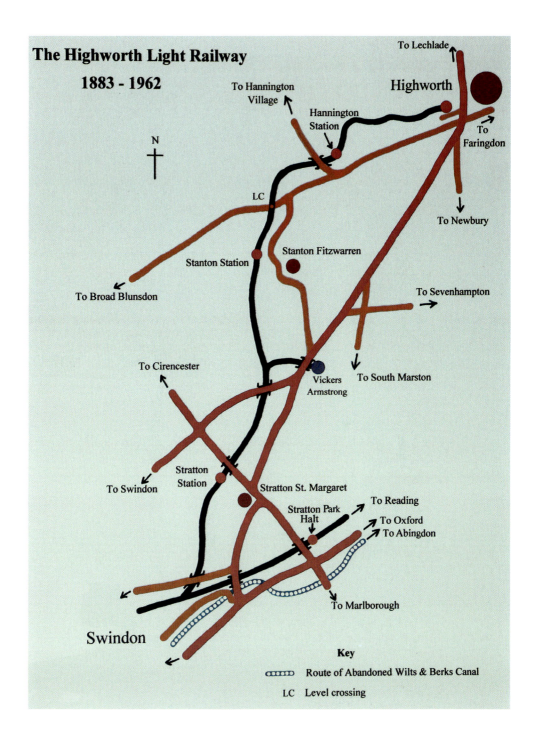

The Highworth Light Railway
1883 - 1962

SWINDON AND HIGHWORTH. (Week Days only.)									63

		G	ⓐ	S		S		G		S	
		a.m.	a.m.	p.m.		p.m.		p.m.		p.m.	
Swindon	dep.	6 0	7 35	12 30	...	4 55	...	5 50	...	6 5	...
Stratton	"	6 7	7 42	12 35	...	5 1	...	5 59	...	6 11	..
Stanton	"	...	...	12 45	...	5 7	...	6 6	...	6 21	...
Hannington	"	ⓐ	8 0	1 1	...	5 16	...	6 19	...	6 34	...
Highworth	arr.	...	8 5	1 6	...	5 21	...	6 24	...	6 39	...

		ⓐ		ⓐ	S	S		
		a.m.		a.m.	p.m.	p.m.		p.m.	
Highworth	dep.	6 47		8 16	1 20	5 43	...	7 10	...
Hannington	"	6 52	Sats. excepted.	8 22	1 26	5 48	...	7 16	...
Stanton	"	7 0		8 30	1 33	5 56	...	7 28	...
Stratton	"	7 6		8 36	1 39	6 1	...	7 35	...
Swindon	arr.	7 16		8 44	1 48	6 10	...	7 45	...

The GWR branch timetable for Swindon to Highworth in 1947. There are only three trains each way on a weekday with the first train of the day from Swindon going to Stratton only. On Saturdays, there are four each way. The timetable for the branch shows a meagre service. In 1952, it was proposed to withdraw the passenger service and it closed on 2 March 1953.

Left: A Highworth branch train in the bay at Swindon with 0-4-2T no 5800 in charge, *c*1958.

Below: Highworth station buildings sometime after closure.

146

Right: An unidentified 0-4-2 tank runs around its train at Highworth, *c*1958. Passenger services had been withdrawn, so this was probably a workmen's train for Swindon Works employees.

Below: Highworth station, *c*1950. (Photo copyright Walter Dendy, deceased, cc-by-sa/2.0)

Chapter 14

The Calne Railway

The Great Western main line through Chippenham, between Paddington and Bristol, opened in 1841 with track to Brunel's broad-gauge standard. There were no plans to connect Calne with Chippenham under the Act of Parliament for the Bristol main line. In the early years of railway building mania, the priority was to connect main centres in one's ideal territory to avoid competition trespass. This was certainly a priority for the Great Western Railway.

Inevitably, the population of Calne, which was not served by a railway, would have felt the disadvantage; a rail link would economise on the transport of goods and make travelling for everyone more comfortable, safer and faster. In response, a group of interested parties held a public meeting in November 1859, proposing to connect Calne with Chippenham with a broad-gauge railway line that was compatible with the GWR line through Chippenham, thus saving on the cost of building their own station in Chippenham and the need for transfer of goods for onward transit.

The scheme was well supported, particularly by the Harris family, owners of the renowned Calne bacon factory, but there were doubts from the GWR that income generated would be insufficient to repay the capital expenditure of the cost of the line for a number of years. This was well founded, as the Calne Railway Company later discovered to its cost.

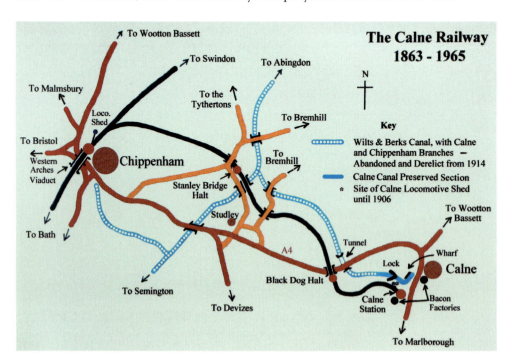

The view east from Chippenham station during realignment of track after the 1965 closure of the Calne branch, which diverged to the right beyond the goods shed in the picture. Note the Hymek diesel-hydraulic in the siding in front of the shed.

A diesel multiple-unit approaches Stanley Bridge Halt (beyond the bridge from which this photograph was taken) c1962.

Black Dog Halt as it appears today, as a feature on the cycle and walkway on the trackbed of the old Calne branch.

A two-coach auto train at Stanley Bridge Halt between Calne and Chippenham. The train is being propelled by a 1400 Class 0-4-2 tank. Note the driver in the operating cab of the leading coach. The driver operates the locomotive from his cab via a system of connected rodding and levers. The fireman remains in the cab of the locomotive, keeping the fire built up to ensure a good head of steam. The locomotive would have been a Swindon-based engine, outbased to Chippenham. The date is c1947, a year before nationalisation. Records show that on 31 December 1947, the possible motive power would have been drawn from a Swindon pool of 1400/33/36/46 or 1453, with either 1433 or 1453 being more likely, as these were subbed to Chippenham.

The engineer appointed for the construction of the line was James Burke, and in November 1859 another engineer, James Samuel, was appointed. James Samuel provided his estimate for construction at £32,000, which was almost £6,000 more than that supplied by James Burke. Upon declaration of this figure, his involvement ceased.

An Act of Parliament was obtained on 15 May 1860, allowing a capital cost of £35,000, but work did not commence on the line until all the shares had been taken up. James Burke had engaged a contractor, Richard Hattersley, to construct the line after negotiation at a cost of £27,000 and an agreement that he would also purchase £10,000 in shares to enable work on the line to commence.

The construction costs and engineer's salary left insufficient funds to purchase a locomotive, so motive power was sought from the GWR, which agreed to supply a single locomotive for two years for a cash sum. Following this arrangement, the supply of motive power would be based upon a percentage of cash receipts.

A year into construction, the costs were overrunning, as civil engineering essentials, such as bridge works and engine and goods shed facilities at Calne, had received insufficient allowance in the estimated costs. Furthermore, the construction of Calne station had previously been agreed as a separate issue, outside of the original estimate.

After a number of failed attempts to open the line, the line was inspected by the Board of Trade on 27 October 1863 and approved to open. The first train was a goods, which included pigs for the bacon factory.

As originally predicted, the income from the line, despite being positive, was insufficient to repay loans. The GWR then advised the Calne Railway that gauge conversion was necessary, and would be undertaken in 1874, at a cost to the GWR. Debts continued to mount, resulting in the line being provisionally sold to the GWR in December 1877, but terms were unacceptable to the shareholders. Eventually agreement was reached and authorised by an Act of Parliament on 28 June 1892.

Calne station in 1904. There is a good trade in milk judging by the number of churns on the platform.

From the opening of the line an arrangement called 'one engine in steam' was in operation, effectively meaning only one engine was allowed on the railway between Chippenham and Calne. This wasn't a problem, as the GWR only supplied one engine for the Calne branch. The single steam engine was housed in a purpose-built engine shed at Calne until 1906.

There had been an engine shed at Chippenham since *c*1858 and I assume the Calne shed was closed and demolished when the branch locomotive was moved to accommodation at Chippenham.

Calne station in 1906.

CHIPPENHAM AND CALNE. (Third class only.)

	Week Days	Sundays
	a.m. a.m. a.m. a.m. a.m. a.m. p.m. p.m. p.m. p.m. p.m. p.m. p.m. p.m. p.m.	a.m. p.m. p.m. p.m.
Chippenham .... dep.	6 15 7 0 8 5 8 43 10 17 11 53 12 48 1 51 3 53 4 30 5 20 6 40 ... 8 30 9 40 10 50	... 10 30 ... 4 50 7 55 10 20 ...
Stanley Bridge Halt ... "	6 21 7 6 . 8 49 10 23 11 59 . 1 57 . 4 36 . 6 46 .. 8 36 9 46 10 56	. 10 36 . 4 56 .
Calne .... arr.	6 30 7 15 8 20 8 58 10 32 12 8 1 0 2 6 3 58 4 45 5 34 6 55 .. 8 45 9 55 11 5	... 10 45 ... 5 5 8 7 10 32 ...
	a.m. a.m. a.m. a.m. a.m. p.m. p.m. p.m. p.m. p.m. p.m. p.m. p.m. p.m. p.m.	a.m. p.m. p.m. p.m.
Calne .... dep.	6 35 7 25 8 25 9 0 10 47 12 20 1 5 2 30 3 15 5 0 5 35 7 5 9 0 10 5 11 10	... 11 5 ... 5 25 8 20 10 40 ...
Stanley Bridge Halt .. "	6 44 7 34 . 9 10 10 56 12 29 1 14 2 39 . 5 9 . 7 14 9 10 14 11 19	... 11 17 . 5 34 .
Chippenham .... arr.	6 50 7 40 8 42 9 17 11 5 12 35 1 21 2 45 3 27 5 15 5 48 7 23 9 15 10 20 11 25	.. 11 23 ... 5 40 8 32 10 52 .

Above: The branch train service from the 1947 GWR timetable. Note the absence of Black Dog Halt, which did not become an official public station until 1952.

Left: Calne goods yard, *c*1905. In the war years, intense activity at the station resulted from the vicinity of Yatesbury and Lyneham airfields.

During the 20th century, a signal box was provided at Calne and an electric train token system introduced. Calne station was enlarged and the main building rebuilt in brick in 1893. In the early 20th century, steam railcars were a feature on the line, until they were withdrawn in the 1930s. They were replaced with 0-4-2 tanks and 0-6-0 panniers. In 1958, diesel multiple-units took over the passenger services. The goods facilities closed in November 1964, a contributing factor being the transfer of bacon factory products to road. After this event, the branch reintroduced the 'one engine in steam' principle.

The last passenger train ran on 18 September 1965 and the track was lifted in 1967. The route has since been used as a cycle track and footpath. It forms part of Sustrans National Cycle route 403.

- Stanley Bridge Halt opened on 3 April 1905 in a rural area of sparse population. The facilities included a short platform and a pagoda-style waiting shelter.
- Black Dog Halt acquired its nameboard on 15 September 1952, when it was made a public station. Previously it was an unofficial stop opened by the Marquis of Lansdown, owner of the Bowood Estate, in c1870. There were no tickets issued until 1952, and the station did not appear in the public timetable until that date.

Above: Calne station in 1965 before closure. By then, the goods yard sidings had been ripped up. A DMU waits for departure time. Note the Harris van in the background.

Right: Calne station in 1964.

The track bed after Stanley Bridge towards Chippenham in 2018.

Chapter 15

The Cheltenham & Great Western Union Railway

The intention of the Cheltenham and Great Western Union Railway (C&GWUR) was to join Cheltenham and Gloucester with Swindon, which would join up with the GWR main line to Bristol and ultimately, Paddington. It was enabled by an Act of Parliament in 1836 with an authorised capital of £750,000. Most of the proposed line was in Gloucestershire, with only the last 11½ miles, from south of Kemble to Swindon, in Wiltshire.

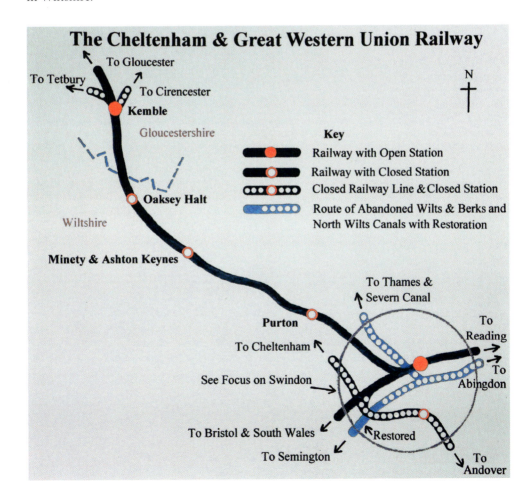

155

Swindon station from the east, *c*1965. Beyond the footbridge are the buildings of Swindon Works, The line to Gloucester, often referred to as 'the Golden Valley Line', takes a right-hand curve between the main offices of the Works and the locomotive shed.

The view over the Gloucester line from the eastern end of Swindon Works in 1981. There are many diesel locomotives in view, mostly 08-type shunters and a number of Class 25 engines. The line of coaches is withdrawn. Swindon station is beyond the curve on the left of the picture.

The line involved a tunnel at Sapperton and a rising gradient of an average of 1 in 75 from Chalford to the summit at Sapperton. The steepest section of the gradient was 1 in 60 for about one mile, and for this section it was intended that stationary steam engines would be required to assist trains on the climb.

The alignment of the C&GWUR between Cheltenham and Gloucester was practically identical to that of the Birmingham and Gloucester Railway, which was approved by an Act of Parliament at the same time as the C&GWUR. It was in each company's interest to collaborate to facilitate joint use of stations. There was, however, the problem of gauge.

The C&GWUR was designed to connect with Brunel's broad gauge at Swindon and it was thus sensible to construct the line from Cheltenham to Swindon in this gauge. As with other major railway ventures, the B&GR was planned in standard gauge. In the circumstances, the C&GWUR agreed, at its expense, to lay an additional rail to enable dual-gauge running on the section concerned, with infrastructure also a joint responsibility.

The C&GWUR was well supported by the GWR, particularly as the construction of the line was in broad gauge. The first stage of the railway took the line into Cirencester via an intended junction at Kemble, which opened for traffic on 31 May 1841. From Kemble, the line was planned to head through a tunnel at Sapperton into the Golden Valley and from there into Gloucester. The route was later known as the Golden Valley Line.

Unfortunately, the C&GWUR ran out of money and was unable to continue construction. The railway had been leased to the GWR, but it sought powers to sell the company to the GWR and to raise further capital to facilitate the sale. The sale was agreed in outline in January 1843, including all the powers and liabilities of the C&GWUR. After an Act of Parliament on 10 May 1844, the line became GWR property.

At the Cheltenham end, the railway opened between Cheltenham and Gloucester as part of the Birmingham and Gloucester Railway on 4 November 1841. A railway was also being constructed between Bristol and Gloucester, so it had been agreed with that company that the GWR would complete the last part of the route between Standish Junction and Gloucester by April 1844, giving running powers to the Bristol and Gloucester Railway.

The GWR failed to complete the line between Kemble and Standish Junction in good time and the construction of the final length into Gloucester was made by the Bristol and Gloucester Railway. The railway fully opened between Swindon and Cheltenham on 12 May 1845.

Kemble opened as an exchange station for Cirencester when the line was fully opened, causing the route to Cirencester to effectively become a branch from a new junction at Kemble. The local people used a station to the north of the interchange called Tetbury Road. In 1872, the line was converted to standard gauge. When Tetbury Road station closed to passengers in 1882 the interchange station at Kemble lost its interchange status and was opened to boarding passengers. Kemble also became the station for a branch to Tetbury in 1889.

In South Wales, the main line through Newport and Cardiff to Swansea was fully opened by July 1852, when it was possible to operate a service between Paddington and South and West Wales using the C&GWUR route between Swindon and Gloucester, which became the Great Western main line to South Wales. This remained as the primary route until the Severn Tunnel opened in 1886.

Within Wiltshire, after Swindon, there were originally two stations; one at Purton and the other at Minety. In 1905, Minety station was renamed Minety and Ashton Keynes. On 18 February 1929, Oaksey was provided with a halt. All these stations closed on 2 November 1964.

Purton station, *c*1910.

5700 Class pannier tank no. 9680 of Swindon shed (82C) slows for Oaksey Halt with a Kemble to Swindon stopping service in 1963.

The first station in Gloucester, a short distance from the Wiltshire border, is Kemble, the one-time junction for Cirencester and Tetbury. It is still open for passengers.

With most of the intermediate stations closed between Swindon and Gloucester in 1964, the line between Swindon and Kemble was singled on 28 July 1968. Traffic has increased since the millennium and the line was restored to double track in September 2013.

The train service from the Wiltshire stations on the Golden Valley Line was never prolific. Purton, for example, had seven trains in the down direction and six up in 1947. Little had changed in 1955 after nationalisation, with the exception that a small number of trains had their destinations extended. Diminutive Oaksey Halt had three trains in each direction on weekdays in 1947, and by 1955 even had one service extended to Hereford.

The 1963 timetable saw the services at the wayside stations severely curtailed; clearly, closure was looming. On 2 November 1964, Purton, Minety and Ashton Keynes and Oaksey Halt all closed.

A4 Pacific 60009 *Union of South Africa* leaves Kemble on 27 October 1994 with the return 'Capital Streak'. The line curving right beside 60009 was the Cirencester branch, which closed in 1965.

Chapter 16

The South Wales Direct Railway

T he original route to South Wales from Paddington left the Bristol line at Swindon, travelling via Stroud, Gloucester and Chepstow to reach Newport, Cardiff and beyond. The Severn Tunnel was opened in 1886, creating a more direct route to South Wales from Paddington via Bristol, Filton and Patchway. This substantially reduced the journey time, but was still not considered direct, at least as far as traffic to London was concerned.

The South Wales coalfield was a significant mining resource in the 19th and the first half of the 20th century. Coal was a significant freight movement to London and Southampton and the GWR had a monopoly. Hostility between the GWR and the Taff Vale, Barry Railway and others started before gauge conversion in 1873. It was difficult prior to this date for onward movement of minerals south into England, from the standard-gauge (then termed narrow-gauge) valley coal lines to the broad-gauge lines of the GWR.

A rival proposal was put forward to construct a new railway line, avoiding GWR involvement to reach the south and south-east. To protect the interests of the GWR, a long-considered direct route to South Wales from Swindon was resurrected.

A bill was eventually placed before Parliament in 1896 and passed on 23 July for a railway line between Wootton Bassett and Patchway. The distance of 30 miles was shorter than the Bristol route by a not insignificant 10 miles. The new route planned for generous curves and less severe gradients than the route via Bristol. A contract was placed with Pearson and Sons Ltd in October 1897, for a sum just shy of £1 million. Major costs on the route were two tunnels, a short length at Alderton of 506 yards and a much longer tunnel at Sodbury of 4,444 yards.

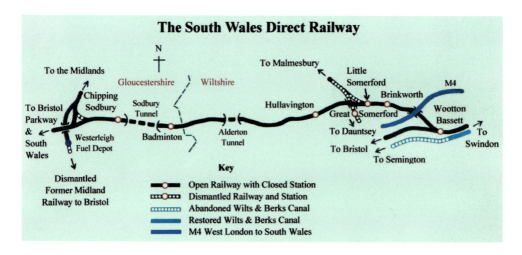

The South Wales Direct Railway opened for goods traffic in sections from 1 January 1903 and fully opened on 1 July for all traffic.

A large marshalling yard was built at Stoke Gifford.

In Wiltshire, stations were built at Brinkworth, Little Somerford, which had four tracks allowing freight and express trains to go through the centre roads (*see* The Malmsbury Railway) and Hullavington.

Other stations were at Badminton, only a little over half a mile from the Wiltshire border with Gloucestershire, Chipping Sodbury, Coalpit Heath and Winterbourne. The South Wales Direct joined the old route to South Wales through Bristol at Patchway, then through the Severn Tunnel which had opened in 1886.

At Stoke Gifford a station was built called Bristol Parkway, which opened in May 1972. At this time, the old Midland route to Bristol, called the Fishponds Line, was closed south of Westerleigh, except for a short stub retained for a fuel depot. The depot can be observed from

Right: **Wootton Bassett station,** *c***1910.**

Below: **Brinkworth station, the first on the South Wales Direct Railway after Wootton Bassett,** *c***1910.**

Castle Class no. 5051 *Earl Bathurst* on the 'St. David's Day Special' passes through the cutting at Hullavington on 1 March 2007. (ST 862 829)

the M4 motorway. A junction at Westerleigh takes the cross-country route to York from Bristol away from the South Wales main line.

The Badminton line passed through rural communities and after World War Two passenger numbers at the wayside stations dropped significantly. All the stations closed in April 1961, with the exception of Badminton, which remained open until June 1968 by arrangement with the Duke of Beaufort. During weekdays in 1963, Badminton had three express trains including the 'Red Dragon' stopping in the down direction.

The goods yards at the stations had all closed by 1965 and the large goods marshalling yard at Stoke Gifford closed in October 1971, making way for Bristol Parkway.

Originally there were plans to install overhead wires all the way to Swansea, but electrification between Cardiff and Swansea has been shelved.

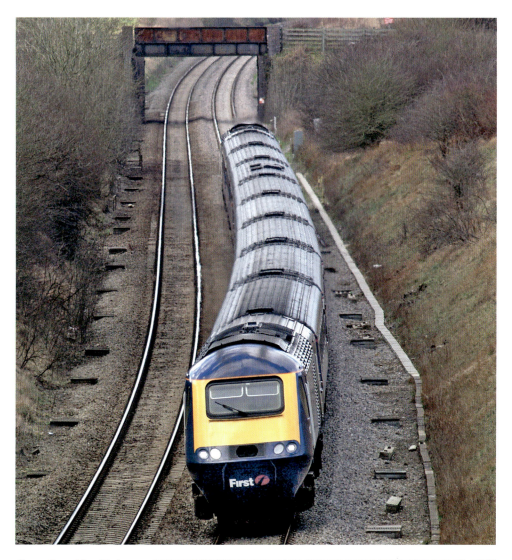

Above: An unidentified HST125 unit weaves its way through Hullavington cutting on 1 March 2007.

Right: Hullavington station, illustrated on a hand-tinted postcard dating from *c*1905.

Although Badminton station is in Gloucestershire, it is only half a mile west of the border with Wiltshire. The scene is intriguing, as a freight seems to be held in the centre road, with the delay for the photograph to be taken causing the locomotive to blow off excess steam. Note that one of the station staff has a shunter's pole in his hand. Photograph taken *c*1906.

Warship Class no. D855 *Triumph* photographed near the Wiltshire border with a train of mixed stock on 29 July 1962.

Chapter 17

The Malmesbury Railway

T he railhead for Malmesbury after the Great Western Railway had built its main line to Bristol was Chippenham, there being a much better highway to this town than Swindon, which was a minor place before Brunel decided to build his railway works there.

At the height of railway mania in the middle of the 19th century, there was an abortive scheme by the Wilts & Gloucestershire Railway, which had connections with both the

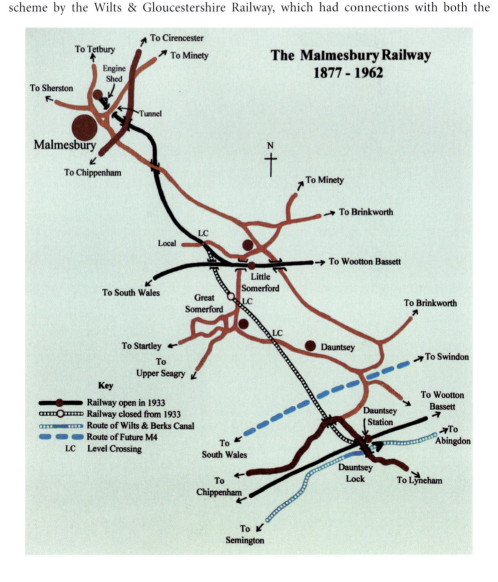

Midland Railway and the GWR, to build a railway from Nailsworth to Christian Malford on the GWR line near Chippenham. Despite an Act of Parliament being passed in July 1864 and some construction work at Malmesbury, disputes between the parties involved could not be resolved.

Eventually a ruling came down on the side of the GWR at the expense of the MR and a Warrant of Abandonment was issued in 1871 for the Wilts & Gloucestershire Railway Company. It is unclear why the W&GR did not seek an agreement with the GWR to continue construction.

Inevitably, the disappointment of townsfolk of their own railway falling at the first hurdle resulted in a scheme being put forward, promoted by the town and GWR, to construct a purely local railway from Dauntsey on the Swindon to Bristol main line into Malmesbury.

This was enthusiastically received and an Act of Parliament was passed on 25 July 1872, on the basis that the GWR and Malmesbury Railway Company subscribe £30,000 each, thus achieving a working arrangement with the GWR, allowing access to Dauntsey station. The engineer for the Malmesbury Railway was named Ward and the appointed contractor was Budd and Holt. Often, they did not see eye to eye. A short tunnel became necessary after the contractor attempted to create a cutting at Holloway on the outskirts of Malmesbury. In addition to the tunnel situation, the construction costs were well on the way to an overspend of £19,000, which the GWR agreed to finance.

In 1876, the GWR appointed its own engineer, Lancaster Owen, who was given overall control, to work with Ward. A further large overspend was projected to complete the line and to settle Budd and Holt's account. This money was raised by local funding loans. The contractors refused to continue working unless their terms of contract were amended.

At this juncture, the shareholders were unhappy at the uncertainty and increasing costs and agreed to sell their shares to the GWR at a loss, but not everyone complied with this arrangement; some held on. However, this did make the GWR the majority shareholder and thus it held the controlling interest and decision making. The agreement with the contractor

Dauntsey station, c1915. The Malmesbury branch platform is beyond the overbridge.

was terminated and GWR completed the line, which was inspected by the board of trade on 20 November 1877 and subsequently opened.

It was always intended that the GWR would operate the line; now, with a controlling interest, there was no doubt this would be the case. The remaining shareholders must have sold their stock to the GWR, or perhaps exchanged for GWR stock sometime previous to 1880, because the Malmesbury Railway was taken over by the GWR by an Act of Parliament in August of that year. The Malmesbury Railway ceased to exist from this point and the line became a branch line of the GWR.

Above: Great Somerford Halt on 26 August 1932.

Right: Holloway Tunnel in 1958, photographed shortly before the terminus at Malmesbury.

Frequent traction on the branch was 0-4-2 tank 5802, sub-shedded at Malmesbury from its home shed of Swindon. Here the engine, which was not auto fitted, is seen outside Malmesbury shed on 18 August 1957.

There was one intermediate station at Great Somerford. It was called Somerford, to attract passengers from both communities of Great Somerford and Little Somerford. In 1903, a direct route to South Wales was opened by the GWR close to Little Somerford, and a new station opened on the route. From that year, Somerford station was renamed Great Somerford. The new station at Little Somerford, situated just half a mile to the north of Great Somerford, caused a reduction of traffic at the old station in passengers and from its small goods yard.

On 22 May 1922, Great Somerford station was given the suffix Halt, which signified a lowering of status. This was after the goods facilities were withdrawn and staffing eliminated, following a significant drop in passenger numbers and freight movement.

With a new main line running much closer to Malmesbury, it was logical to provide a connection at Little Somerford. This would have the effect of shortening route mileage of the branch from 6½ miles to 3¾ miles. It is surprising that it took 30 years to effect this change, bearing in mind the potential savings in running costs.

In July 1933, a link was opened and the line between Dauntsey and the junction with the new link closed. This included Great Somerford Halt. However, for a short time, the track from Dauntsey was used as a siding. This arrangement was soon changed to the northern end of the line, from the new junction to Great Somerford on the old branch formation. This was also operated as a siding, with a ground frame at the junction. It was used for redundant wagon storage until 1959. South of Great Somerford, the branch track was lifted by 1949.

Little Somerford station, *c*1958. The Malmesbury branch line veered right after the signal box. There was no bay platform for the branch. (The Wiltshire and Swindon History Centre)

The Gloucestershire Railway Society ran a tour on the Malmesbury branch in 1962, hauled by 1600 Class 1658. Here it stands in the closed station at Malmesbury.

Malmesbury station just after the turn of the 20th century. The train in the platform is for Dauntsey and probably hauled by a Class 517 0-4-2 tank. Malmesbury Abbey takes a prominent spot at the top of the town.

Dauntsey station was retained for passengers on the Swindon to Chippenham route until closure on 4 January 1965. The station accommodated branch trains until 1933 from a bay built on the western end of the up platform, by extending the platform beyond an overbridge. Track was retained in the bay until 1956, possibly being used as a head shunt until the old track of the branch was removed.

Malmesbury station was situated beyond the town via a 105-yard tunnel. It is probable that the location of the station was influenced by groundwork started by the Wilts & Gloucestershire Railway, then aborted. Remember that Malmesbury would have been an intermediate station on a through route of the proposed W&GR and the station site may have been partially prepared. The station had a goods yard with a shed and cattle dock. There was a single platform with run-round facilities.

By rail, Malmesbury was about 22 miles from Swindon, from where the locomotives were supplied to operate the line. To avoid light engine movements to refuel, the station yard had its own single road engine shed with a coaling platform and water tower over. The diminutive shed acted as a sub-shed to Swindon. Typically in the 1940s/'50s the allocation was one 0-4-2 tank.

The branch was worked by one engine in steam and, upon opening, there were six trains a day each way. The frequency increased up to World War Two with the odd through working to Swindon and return. The frequency declined when bus services improved to major centres from Malmesbury, including Swindon and Chippenham. Travelling to Chippenham by rail involved changing trains. The passenger service on the branch soon became unprofitable and the station closed in September 1951. Goods facilities were retained until November 1962.

LITTLE SOMERFORD AND MALMESBURY. (Week Days only.)																					
	a.m.	a.m.			p.m.	p.m.	p.m.	p.m.					a.m.	a.m.				p.m.	p.m.	p.m.	p.m.
Little Somerford dep.	8 0	11 53	...	...	2 45	6 3	7 3	9 8 32	} D		Malmesbury .... dep.	7 21	11 30	...	...		2 23	5 35	6 30	7 8 35	} D
Malmesbury .. . arr.	8 8	12 1	.	.	2 53	6 11	7 11	9 8 40			Little Somerford arr.	7 30	11 39	.	.		2 32	5 44	6 39	7 8 34	

The 1947 branch timetable shows six trains a day each way, with the last service of the day, a through train to Swindon and return, on Saturdays only. This train allowed two hours in town before its return.

Goods handled at Malmesbury were coal, general merchandise and agricultural machinery. Founded in 1870, Ratcliffe and Son made machinery for agricultural purposes and must have used the goods facilities for transportation before road transport became more economical. At Great Somerford, before closure in 1922, milk in churns was a major source of income, with incoming coal and agricultural feed making the goods yard viable.

Malmesbury station yard is now a car park for the town and the only evidence that the site was once a station is the retention of the engine shed building as a garage.

Above: **The old engine shed is retained as a tyre exchange garage.**

Below: **The track layout of Malmesbury station as depicted on a plaque erected on the old engine shed in 2010 by Malmsbury Civic Trust. The passenger trains into Malmesbury from Little Somerford had the affectionate name of 'The Malmsbury Bunk'.**

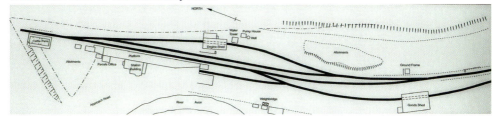

Chapter 18

Wilts, Somerset & Weymouth Railway with Bradford to Bathampton

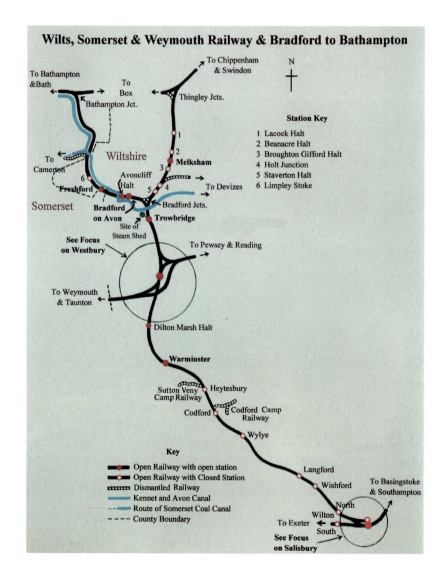

There was intense rivalry between railway companies during the early years of railway construction in Britain. This particularly applied between the London and South Western Railway and the Great Western. It was in the interests of the main players to help finance smaller companies, thereby having a say in their futures and to prevent trespass into territories each company considered their own.

The L&SWR was keen to spread into Great Western territory and proposed a railway between Basingstoke and Swindon, which met with intense opposition from the GWR, as Swindon was considered the beating heart of the company, with a principal railway works under construction, to be completed in 1845. The L&SWR proposal did not gain favour, but a scheme to create a railway from Chippenham to Weymouth received more support.

There were plans for the Bristol and Exeter Railway to open a railway to Weymouth, but this scheme failed to materialise. So, promoted by the GWR, a company called the Wilts, Somerset and Weymouth Railway (WS&WR) obtained Parliamentary powers in 1845 to build a railway from the Swindon to Bristol main line at Thingley, west of Chippenham, to Weymouth and Salisbury. The Bristol main line had been opened in 1841 in broad gauge and the WS&WR, influenced by the GWR, was also planned in the wide gauge.

The WS&WR would be the lessee of the Weymouth line from the GWR and would subscribe half of the capital required. Support to build the line was on the proviso that the GWR would connect Bath with Bradford on Avon, creating a connection with the WS&WR at a future Bradford Junction. Powers for the construction of this line were sought in 1846.

The Kennet and Avon Canal Company was concerned that railway progress would take trade away from the canal and sought to be part of the expanding railway network. Such a scheme was doomed to failure.

The 1845 Act of Parliament permitted branches to be constructed from the principal route from Thingley Junction to Weymouth, to Bradford on Avon, Devizes, Sherbourne plus a coal branch to Radstock from Frome. The Sherbourne branch was never built as the main LSWR line to Exeter ran through the town. Nor did a branch to Bradford materialise, despite a prepared

A Swindon to Westbury service has just left the Bristol main line at Thingley Junction heading south for Melksham. The unit is a Class 158, no. 158888, photographed on 24 February 2018. (ST 902 704)

formation at a potential Bradford North Junction, due to a shortage of funds. However, the GWR connection to reach the WS&WR was planned to take in the town of Bradford on Avon.

The first section of the WS&WR to be built was between Thingley Junction and Westbury. This was via the wool towns of Melksham and Trowbridge and was opened on 2 September 1848 as a broad-gauge railway, but converted to standard in 1874.

There was a strange arrangement at Thingley Junction to access the WS&WR line from the Bristol line. Although standard procedure now, facing junctions were banned in the early years of railways. This was because trains could be switched by inexperienced hands, or in error, from a fast line to a slow line or dead-end siding, with potentially disastrous results. At Thingley Junction, WS&WR trains passed over a trailing point on the main line and reversed back into a siding, before moving forward again on to the WS&WR metals. After the practice of signal interlocking was introduced, facing junctions were considered safe and the former procedure was discontinued.

It was important to raise the money promised for construction to continue beyond Westbury. This proved difficult and revenue from passenger receipts had barely started before the WS&WR was in financial drought. There was only one option available; to sell its interests to its backers, the GWR. The decision was made in December 1849 and the business transferred on 14 March 1850. An Act of Parliament dissolved the WS&WR on 3 July 1851. Further construction was carried out by the GWR directly.

The present track between Thingley and Bradford Junction is now a single-track by-way, with a passenger service between Westbury and Swindon and a few stone trains from and to the Somerset quarries and departmental trains from Westbury yard.

In 1848, the only station on this section was at Melksham, as is the case today. However, it is a shadow of its former self, being a short single platform constructed on some of the remains of the old down platform.

Lacock Halt, *c*1965.

The opening day for Lacock Halt on 16 October 1905. Railmotor no. 56 on its inaugural run on the line is supported by a saddle tank.

When the era of pick-up goods ceased in the 1960s, the goods yards closed at most stations, and at Melksham in 1964. Beeching cuts closed the station in 1966 and the buildings were soon demolished. However, the line remained open, being singled in 1967 as far as Bradford South Junction. Fortunes changed in May 1985, when the station reopened, at first with a nominal service, but soon expanded to six trains a day each way between Westbury and Swindon.

In 1905, two Halts opened between Thingley and Melksham; Lacock and Beanacre. At Lacock, in 1942, during World War Two, sidings were laid for the Air Ministry. At the same time, a west loop was laid at Thingley Junction, known as the Air Ministry Loop. This closed in 1959 and was removed, but the sidings at Lacock lasted until 1964.

It is interesting to consider that if the Air Ministry Loop had been installed considerably earlier, trains would have been able to reach Weymouth from Bristol via Thingley Junction, giving less credence to a line through the Avon valley, although as a shorter route it would have eventually been built anyway.

Beanacre Halt was similar in size to Lacock Halt, but was barely used and closed ahead of Lacock in 1955.

After Melksham, another Halt was opened in 1905, at Broughton Gifford. This also failed to attract passengers in any volume and closed in 1955.

The branch to Devizes was completed in 1857 and from 1862, when the Berks and Hants Extension was completed; through traffic was possible via a new station at Holt Junction. This was an island platform and opened in 1861, but at first was a transfer point between trains using the main line of the WS&WR and the branch. In 1874, it was opened to passengers from the village, a path and station access being provided.

Goods facilities were opened at Holt Junction in 1877 and closed in 1963. The station was closed along with the Devizes branch in 1966.

Another Halt was opened in 1905 at Staverton and fared rather better than Beanacre and Broughton Gifford, but was also closed in 1966.

Melksham station looking north, c1910.

I have already mentioned that a bed for the track at a potential Bradford North Junction had been made by 1848, but not laid with rails to reach Bradford on Avon as originally intended.

In 1893, track was laid on this triangle to create a junction with the line constructed along the Avon Valley at a new Bradford West Junction. It was thus possible, between 1893 and 1966, for trains to run from Reading via the Berks and Hants and Devizes to Bath and Bristol, and it could also act as a diversionary route in the event of closure of the Bristol main line through Swindon.

By 1967, there were no stations open between Thingley Junction and Trowbridge and the line was singled north of Bradford South Junction. The rarely used Bradford North to West loop was singled in 1967, closed in March 1990 and subsequently removed. At Bradford South Junction, the line from Thingley Junction joins the route between Bathampton, Weymouth and Salisbury, which has become the primary link between the Bristol main line and the south.

The new station at Melksham, photographed in February 2018. (ST 900 645)

Holt Junction on 4 July 1905. A Portsmouth-bound excursion is arriving at the station. The passengers fill the platform and I wonder if it is a works outing. Note the fully laden goods train waiting for the road.

Holt Junction station, photographed after it closed in 1966.

Staverton Halt shortly after closure in 1966.

Left: The 10.24 Swindon to Weymouth service, composed of diesel multiple-unit set P460, was photographed near Staverton on 31 March 1988.

Below: The railway scene looking north from the Kennet and Avon aqueduct over the railway at Bradford South Junction on 8 November 2017. The unit is 158766, forming a Westbury to Swindon service, and is about to enter the single line to Thingley Junction.

The engineer for this link was Isambard Kingdom Brunel, who chose a route through the Avon valley following the river and Kennet and Avon Canal. This was a simple choice, because the contours were favourable and avoided adverse gradients.

Starting in the historic county of Somerset at Bathampton Junction on the Bristol to Swindon main line, the railway sweeps south past Claverton, with the canal on the right and the river on the left, effectively sandwiched between the two watercourses. About a quarter of a mile south of passing under Dundas Aqueduct, the tracks enter Wiltshire, the canal now on the left-hand side of the railway.

In 1847, progress on the Thingley to Westbury line was achieving good momentum and indeed some infrastructure at Bradford on Avon was complete in 1848 by the GWR, but with no rails. In the same year, the WS&WR had reached Westbury. After that company ran out of finance, the GWR took on the remainder of the civil engineering to reach Salisbury, Weymouth and Radstock. This must have taken effort away from the Bathampton line, which resulted in a Writ of Mandamus being issued in 1852 by the court, requiring the GWR to meet its obligations to complete the connecting line through the Avon Valley. Mandamus, in Latin, simply translates as 'we command'. Despite this command, the line was not open until 1857, due to construction difficulties, as the line had to navigate a route under two aqueducts that carry the Kennet and Avon Canal across the valley.

The first station on the line after Bathampton was Limpley Stoke, opened in 1857. This was the junction for the Camerton branch. Although divergence from the Bathampton route was north of the station near Dundas Aqueduct, such that only the junction itself is in Wiltshire, the remainder of the branch was in Somerset. Limpley Stoke station was a casualty of the Beeching cuts and closed in 1966. There was a small yard handling stone from local quarries until 1960. The station building still exists, complete with a reproduction station name-board, and is now private.

The Camerton branch was built in 1910, mostly on the bed of the old Somerset Coal Canal, which became disused after the railways took the coal traffic generated by the Somerset coalfield. Near the one-time railway junction are the preserved truncated remains of the coal

Limpley Stoke station, *c*1910.

The remains of Limpley Stoke station, seen from a lane below the railway line in 2016. (ST 783 612) The old station is private property and there is no access.

canal where it joins the Kennet and Avon at Dundas. This is Brassknocker Basin. Wiltshire cannot claim this attraction, as it is sited over the border in Somerset.

The Camerton branch traffic was primarily coal, but passengers were carried between Hallatrow and Limpley Stoke, with an eight-year blip, until 1925. The coal traffic declined with pit closures and the line closed in 1951.

The branch is most famous for the film *The Titfield Thunderbolt*, which featured 14xx Class 1401 and Liverpool and Manchester locomotive *Lion*. The film was a comedy released in 1953 about a group of villagers trying to keep their branch line open against all odds.

The locomotive used in *The Titfield Thunderbolt*, 14xx Class 1401, at Swindon, *c*1955.

Freshford station, seen from the towpath of the Kennet and Avon Canal in October 2017. (ST 793 600)

Between Limpley Stoke and the next station at Freshford, there were loops and sidings added in 1910 to cater for wagon storage and coal from the Camerton branch for onward transit. Siding and loops had been removed by 1964. Freshford station opened with the line in 1857 and survived the Beeching axe. The original station buildings no longer exist and have been replaced with modern station shelters. Strictly speaking, this station is in the historic county of Somerset, being situated on a projecting stub of Somerset from the village of Freshford. However, it is included for completeness.

Standing close to Avoncliff Aqueduct, the station of Avoncliff opened as a Halt on 9 July 1906. On 5 May 1969, the Halt suffix was dropped. It is believed that Avoncliff escaped closure in 1966 under the Beeching cuts due to poor road access to the hamlet.

The station was a request stop until July 2010 and now trains are scheduled to stop in not less than hourly intervals in each direction. For a small place, the station has respectable passenger figures, helped by tourism to a popular destination. To change platforms, it is necessary to use the aqueduct path to cross the lines.

Bradford on Avon station was originally to have been a branch from the WS&WR. The intended junction south of Bradford did not receive its track until 1895, long after the station opened with through trains to Bathampton. The station dates from 1848 and represents an iconic Isambard Brunel design, resembling a lodge of a country estate house in mellow Bath stone. Upon opening, there were five trains a day in each direction.

Class 33 no. 33064 near Freshford with the Cardiff to Portsmouth service on 23 March 1988.

The goods station closed in 1964 and the station signal box was demolished in 1966. The land they occupied is a large car park for the station and town.

The line passes through a 159-yard tunnel shortly after Bradford station, then passes Bradford South Junction to join the original route of the Wilts, Somerset and Weymouth Railway before going under the Kennet and Avon Canal to the outskirts of Trowbridge. Trowbridge was opened in 1848 as part of the WS&WR main line. It was a substantial station, but after the canopied structures were considered unsafe in 1984 and were demolished, it was rebuilt in a much simpler and more modern form. It is still significant in terms of passenger numbers, with almost one million per annum. Before closure of the Devizes branch, there were through services from Paddington terminating there.

Avoncliff Halt in 1960. A freight from South Wales, hauled by 3837, heads for Salisbury.

Hymek no. D7016, with a freight, approaches Bradford on Avon in 1965.

Castle Class no. 5057 *Earl Waldegrave* with a Cardiff to Portsmouth freight near Bradford on Avon on 14 October 1963.

Class 33 no. 33021 leaves Bradford on Avon with a Portsmouth to Cardiff service on 12 February 1988. (ST 820 606)

Class 33 no. 33001 approaches Bradford on Avon with the 09.50 Swansea to Portsmouth on 26 February 1988. (ST 820 606)

The last day of Class 33s on Cardiff to Portsmouth services on 14 May 1988 with nos. 33112 *Templecombe* and 33026.

The 'Cathedrals Express' to Bristol at Bradford on Avon with 70000 *Britannia* on 12 April 2012. (ST 622 606)

Bradford on Avon station on 16 October 2014. (ST 826 607)

The goods yard had a broad-gauge goods shed, which became disused in the 1960s. It should have been made a listed structure and protected for posterity, but became unsafe in 1985 and was demolished. On the opposite side of the track, a locomotive shed was built in 1875. This had three 100ft roads, and in 1901 was noted to house an allocation of 26 engines, mostly of 0-6-0 wheel arrangement in both tender and tank types.

The loco shed closed in 1923 after Westbury shed opened in 1915. The building remained in use as a carriage and wagon repair and storage shed for a number of years after the locomotives moved out, and was noted still standing in 1960.

Above: Class 33 no. 33019 approaches Bradford South Junction from the south with a service for Cardiff.

Left: Trowbridge station complex *c*1908. The broad-gauge goods shed can be seen in the goods yard. The engine shed is in the left background.

Hall Class no. 5910 *Park Hall* at Trowbridge shortly before departure on 3 September 1958, probably to Bristol and Cardiff, as the locomotive was allocated to Bristol Bath Road at the time.

Trowbridge station in 1905.

Trowbridge after rebuilding, 22 March 2018. In the station is Sprinter 150130 with another unidentified Sprinter unit leading on a Gloucester service. (ST 852 579)

The line proceeds south out of Trowbridge and negotiates Hawkeridge Junction to reach Westbury station. Westbury as a rail centre is examined in the chapter 'Focus on Westbury'. The line divides at Westbury – south to Salisbury and west to Fairwood Junction where the Westbury avoiding line joins to head for Frome.

The county boundary with Somerset is about midway between Westbury and Frome.

Frome has an avoiding line between Clink Road Junction and Blatchbridge Junction. Frome station had an overall roof on my last visit, but the track has been singled. Here the Radstock line diverged and is still used by stone traffic from Whatley Quarry onward through Frome and Westbury. The WS&WR reached Frome in 1850 and Radstock in 1854.

After the GWR took over the construction of the route miles planned by the WS&WR in 1850, progress to Warminster on the Salisbury route was rapid and arrived in 1851.

If one stands on the platform end at Westbury, the bank curving south after South Junction is clearly visible. This is Dilton Bank, and has an average rising gradient out of Westbury of 1 in 73. The gradient rises for 2½ miles from Westbury South Junction. Banking engines were often required for heavy freights on this incline. The locomotives involved in banking duties would fall back at Warminster and return to Westbury when the road was clear.

In 1937, a small halt was built with wooden sleepers called Dilton Marsh Halt. The Halt suffix was removed in 1969.

Warminster station opened on 9 September 1851 as the short-term terminus of the Salisbury branch of the WS&WR. At least it was supposed to be short term, but the remainder of the line into Salisbury was not complete until 30 June 1856. There were no severe gradients to cope with; generally, it was a rising gradient all the way from Salisbury to Warminster with only short stretches of less the 1 in 125.

Originally, Warminster had a train shed covering the platforms and tracks, with a footbridge that was also covered. The train shed roof was removed c1930 and the footbridge roof much later. Awnings were added to the station buildings, which are not in keeping with the original wooden buildings, being basic and undecorated as with most other Great Western designed stations. The original station buildings are part of the Warminster Heritage Blue Plaque Trail.

An unidentified 57xx pannier tank at Hawkeridge Junction with a Trowbridge to Frome train on 10 August 1964.

Pannier 4673 comes into Westbury from the Frome line. The coal wagon suggests the train would have originated on the Radstock branch on 10 April 1964.

Left: Dilton Marsh Halt, *c*1960.

Below: Modified Hall 6963 *Throwley Hall* climbs Dilton Bank out of Westbury with a freight on 25 March 1963.

Bottom: Class 50 no. 50149 *Defiance* on a test freight at Upton Scudamore on 18 October 1987. The engine had been modified with lower-geared bogies to work freight trains in Cornwall. It only carried this number and freight livery for two years before it reverted to 50049.

Above and below: Warminster station, *c*1968. Note there is an upper quadrant signal at the end of the platform, which must have replaced a GWR lower quadrant around this time.

Close to the station was a Geest banana depot with its own siding. Trains of box vans specifically designed for banana traffic came from the docks at Southampton and Bristol to the depot for distribution. The siding was removed by 1980.

There was always a strong military presence at Warminster and the sidings near the station for military purposes reflected this, particularly during the war years. Goods services at Warminster were withdrawn in April 1973 and the station sidings eventually removed. It is difficult to imagine today that there was ever a goods yard at the station.

Left: Warminster station exterior in 2014. (ST 877 453)

Below: The interior of the station has barely changed in 50 years, but the gas-type station lamp standards and large station name-board have been removed.

Class 66 no. 66016 with the morning Westbury to Eastleigh departmental engineer's train comes into Warminster station, passing a Cardiff-bound diesel unit on 30 September 2014. (ST 877 453)

Class 59 no. 59205 *L. Keith McNair* northbound with empty stone boxes near Bishopstrow on 12 April 2007. (ST 903 445)

South of Warminster, the next station was Heytesbury, but the line passes through Bishopstrow and close to Norton Bavant prior to reaching the village. Here there are good photographic opportunities as the line is visible from the Warminster Road.

Heytesbury opened for goods traffic on 11 June 1856 and for passengers later that month. The station was fairly basic, but the yard had a goods shed. All facilities were withdrawn on 18 September 1955 and the buildings demolished, with the exception of the main station building, which still stands but without access.

The main feature of Heytesbury was the branch to Sutton Veny Camp, which diverged left from the main line just north of the station. It was opened in 1916 for trains to the camp hospital. The line was 3½ miles long. All track and the hospital were removed in 1926.

A significant factor in the demise of Heytesbury station was its location, over half a mile down a lane from the village. Once public road transport became a feature of rural life, train passengers diminished. However, there was another factor; a decline in the rural population, with villagers moving out to seek employment in the more urbanised areas of Wiltshire.

Between Heytesbury and the next station site at Codford, there is a level crossing at Upton Lovell. Before 1982, it was manually operated, but automatic half barriers were fitted, eliminating the need for a ground frame crossing box. Soon after the crossing, the line reaches Codford, some way out of the village. Its original single platform opened in June 1856, but a passing loop, together with a second platform, were constructed in 1897. The line was doubled in the Heytesbury direction in 1899 and towards Wylye in 1900. Closure for passengers took place on 19 September 1955 and the goods yard closed on 10 June 1963.

A diverted northbound Freightliner comes through Norton Bavant with Class 66 no. 66555. (ST 910 438)

Heytesbury station *c*1916. No footbridge was provided and passengers crossed on the barrow crossing.

During 1914, an army camp was built at Codford for Anzac soldiers training for the Western Front. The camp was served by a 2¾-mile branch line veering to the right north of the station platforms. The branch was closed in 1922 and lifted.

During the soldiers' stay at the camp, a rising sun badge was cut into the chalk hillside. It is still visible from the A36 south of the village. The badge, along with war graves in the village churchyard, many as the result of a flu pandemic, are the only reminders of World War One Anzac soldiers and the regard the local community had for them.

A freight hauled by 66025 passes the old Heytesbury station building on 13 April 2007. (ST 923 419)

Class 33 no. 33051 with a Portsmouth to Cardiff train on 12 April 1988. The photograph was taken on the southern side of the lane road bridge, next to the site of Heytesbury station. On the right of the picture was a refuge siding protected by its own ringed goods signal. Both were removed in December 1961.

After Codford, the railway twists through Sherrington, an ideal photographic location for up trains, through the Wylye Valley and under the notorious bottlenecked A303, to the village of Wylye. When the station was opened here in 1856 and until 1874, it was spelt Wiley.

There is a level crossing just beyond the station site, which was given barriers in 1973 and subsequently automated, at which time the signal box closed.

During World War Two, there was an RAF munitions store in Grovelley Wood, a stretch of woodland on high ground overlooking the Wylye Valley. This was serviced by extra sidings at Wylye, which were in use until 1951. Goods facilities were withdrawn from Wylye on 2 October 1961, the passenger service having been withdrawn on 19 September 1955.

Originally single track, the Salisbury branch of the WS&WR had been doubled by the end of 1901. The section towards Salisbury out of Wylye station was doubled in March of the same year.

During my research into the WS&WR, I was surprised to learn that there was a station at Langford to serve the parishes of Little Langford and Steeple Langford and the hamlet of Hanging Langford. It was very short lived, being opened with the line on 30 June 1856 and closed in October 1857. Evidence of the station's existence can be found at the website *British History Online*. It states: 'The Salisbury Warminster section of the GWR was made across the parish [Little Langford] very near the turnpike road in 1856: the nearest station was at Hanging Langford in Steeple Langford until 1857, afterwards at Great Wishford until 1955.'

Wishford station was situated in the village of Great Wishford, or Wishford Magna, as it was known in the past. Wishford had a goods yard with goods shed and cattle dock, the dock being a later addition to the facilities. The station and goods yard were closed from 19 September 1955, leaving the nearest goods facilities at Wylye or Wilton North.

Codford station, c1910.

The Codford Camp Railway during World War One. The scene shows Camp no. 6 near the extremity of the branch.

This scene at Sherrington is reminiscent of American railroads, where trains are half a mile long and pulled by three or more locomotives. The train is a departmental engineer's between Westbury and Eastleigh on 16 January 2012, hauled by Class 66 nos. 66200, 66132 and 66068. (ST 966 389)

Black 5 no. 44932 passing Wylye with a Waterloo to Bristol excursion on 11 March 2012. (SU 004 376)

Top: Wylye station, *c*1912. Note the motor car in the station forecourt and the milk churns on the platform.

Above: Class 66 no. 66075 catches the late afternoon sun with tanks from Fawley to Plymouth through Little Langford on 2 February 2007. (SU 078 355)

Below: Class 66 no. 66097 seen at Hanging Langford with an empty engineer's train to Eastleigh on 31 January 2007. (SU 033 368)

Class 59 no. 59204 heads south through Great Wishford with Mendip Rail box wagons in February 2007. (SU 049 365)

Wilton North station opened with the line in 1856, although the suffix was not used until 1949, when the former LSWR station was renamed Wilton South. North station closed in 1955, but South didn't close until 1966. The goods yard at North station remained in use until 6 September 1965. Some buildings still exist in alternative use.

In 2015, the Trans-Wilts Community Rail Partnership proposed a new station to be called Wilton Parkway or more recently Stonehenge and Wilton Junction. This proposal situates the station to the south-east of the old station site of North Wilton.

In 1972, connection was made to the English China Clays' quarry at Quidhampton with the GWR route into Salisbury. Another quarry was situated at East Grimstead on the Romsey

Wishford station from an old postcard, *c*1910. A down train for Salisbury is about to stop.

Merchant Navy 35028 *Clan Line* hauls the Venice Simplon Orient Express Pullman stock through the Wylye Valley towards Great Wishford on 14 March 2007. The view is towards Wilton. (SU 082 345)

line from Salisbury. This had a rail connection, but road access was more restricted as the quarry was situated on a byway surrounded by lanes. Transfer trains ran from this quarry to Quidhampton.

In 1973, a junction with the former LSWR route was introduced just east of Wilton, where the former GWR and LSWR routes converged. The old GWR route was closed into Salisbury, but the Quidhampton quarry sidings were serviced with a retained link. Up to this date there were two parallel double-track railways running into Salisbury. The GWR route terminated in its own terminus at Fisherton (see Salisbury in Focus).

Wilton North on 4 July 1963. Wilton South, the LSWR station, was a short distance south of North station. In 1901, neither station had a compass point suffix at the time.

60019 *Bittern* running as 4492 passes the proposed site of Wilton Parkway station with the 'Bath Spa Express' on 30 August 2011. (SU 101 319)

Standard Class 5 no. 73014 runs into Salisbury from the Former GWR route with a train from Cardiff, *c*1960.

Chapter 19

Focus on Westbury

A railway first reached Westbury in 1848 with the terminus of the Wilts, Somerset & Weymouth Railway from Chippenham. The railway was originally intended to reach Weymouth and Salisbury, with a junction of lines at Westbury. This company soon met financial difficulties and sold its enterprise to the GWR in 1850.

Under the GWR, construction continued apace and westward to Frome, which opened in October 1850, and towards Salisbury, as far as Warminster, in September 1851. Another line north to Bathampton was opened in 1857, from the original WS&WR line at Bradford South Junction to join the GWR main line to Bristol and the West. This was in broad gauge until conversion in 1874 to standard gauge.

Until 1900, trains reached Westbury from the Berks and Hants extension line via Devizes, but following the construction of the Stert to Westbury Railway, which opened in that year, distance and journey times to Westbury and Weymouth were shortened.

After the Castle Cary to Cogload Junction line was constructed and opened in 1906, the Berks and Hants route to Exeter and the west via Castle Cary was in direct competition with the London & South Western route to Exeter via Axminster.

Beyond Exeter there was only one winner to Plymouth, as the L&SWR took a circuitous route through the north of Devon. Westbury became an important junction, but less so after the Westbury avoiding line was constructed in 1933.

Before the Stert and Westbury line was built, Westbury station was re-modelled in 1899 in preparation for increased traffic. Two island platforms, each 600ft long and 40ft wide, were constructed. Between 1899 and today, the station has been remodelled a number of times, but the basic island platform layout has remained.

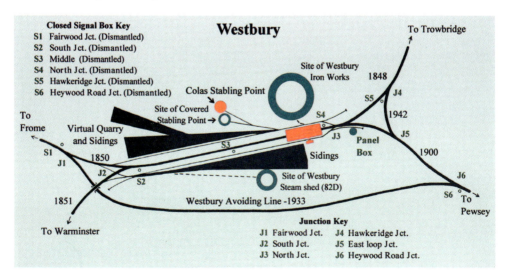

Westbury station about 1904. An 0-4-2 tank is in the up platform with a long rake of coaches, probably for the Bristol line. Note the iron works to the rear.

In 1968, Westbury Middle Signal Box was closed and track and signal modifications were made to allow North and South boxes to control the station, yards and junctions in the central area.

In May 1984, Westbury Panel Box was opened, the manual signal boxes closed and the station re-signalled. About this time, the down Salisbury line platform was taken out of commission and the track lifted.

Another view of the station from the platform, *c*1908.

Westbury Iron Works, situated adjacent to the station, in 1906.

Westbury White Horse, station and old water-filled iron workings.

Hall Class no. 6952 *Leighton Hall* leaves Westbury, passing North Signal Box, with the 17.35 to Swindon on 12 August 1964.

Westbury Iron Works was opened in 1857 and two blast furnaces installed in 1858, after the adjacent GWR station had been well established for 10 years. The railway's presence certainly helped the viability of the project to exploit the iron ore beds to the north of the town. The iron ore was quarried by opencast methods and transported to the furnaces on tramways. The heyday of the works was in the early 1870s. In 1872 the weekly production of pig iron was 400 tons, at which time the plant employed 200 people. The business declined towards the end of the century and was shut in 1901, only to reopen two years later. During World War One, the business thrived with the war effort, but stopped smelting in 1920.

56xx Class no. 6682 heads a Radyr to Southampton coal train out of Westbury on 2 December 1963.

Mogul 6372 with the RCTS 'Wessex Wyvern' Railtour on 8 July 1956, taking a breather in Westbury.

Modified Hall 6999 *Capel Dewi Hall* leaves Westbury on the Salisbury line with loaded cement wagons for Poole on 4 January 1964.

'Flying Pig' 43047 comes off the Trowbridge line passing North Junction with a freight on 18 August 1964. Possibly running in after a spell in Swindon Works.

County Class no. 1011 *County of Chester* approaches Hawkeridge Junction en route to Bath on 4 April 1964.

Until 1915, the Westbury area's steam shed was at Trowbridge, but in April of that year, a new depot was opened, known by the Great Western under the coding of WBY, in the Bristol locomotive division. After nationalisation in 1948, the coding was changed to follow the old LMS tradition of numbers and letters and became 82D. The division top shed at Bristol Bath Road became 82A.

Shortly before nationalisation, there were 71 locomotives allocated, of which 20 were mixed traffic and passenger 4-6-0s, ten heavy freight 2-8-0 engines and other sundry classes. Local freight trips and yard shunting duties were handled by nine panniers and four auto-fitted panniers used for shuttle trips.

By 1959, the allocation had fallen to 53, consisting of 13 mixed traffic 4-6-0s, two heavy freight 2-8-0s, various moguls and tanks, but the pannier allocation had increased to 19 and there were still four auto-fitted panniers.

In 1963, the depot was re-coded 83C and by 1965 only eight panniers were allocated. The depot closed in September 1965 and the six remaining panniers went for scrap. Diesel power had superseded steam.

Above: Westbury engine shed *c*1946 and, inset, the locomotive shed code for Westbury used after nationalisation.

Right: Modified Hall 6991 *Acton Burnell Hall* stands by the coaling plant on 19 October 1963.

Castle Class no. 7026 *Tenby Castle* being manually turned on the turntable at Westbury shed on 11 August 1964.

56xx Class no. 6625 in Westbury shed yard in 1958.

A small covered stabling point for diesels took over from the steam shed, with stabling room to its exterior. The locomotives were generally used for stone traffic to and from Westbury's virtual quarry sidings on the up side of the yard and mainly general departmental traffic in the down yard. To this day, this practice continues, but is more streamlined, with the main train locomotive shunting wagons before it sets off for its destination.

The depot was dismantled, sometime after 1990, but the sidings are still used for stabling, mainly Colas-liveried Class 70s and multiple units. The yard sees a variety of freight company locos, the liveries becoming increasingly colourful.

Pannier no. 4607 and three others inside the shed in 1965.

Class 56 no. 56042 inside the diesel shed at Westbury on 25 June 1989. Four other members of the class are stabled outside.

Above: In July 1976, Diesel Hydraulic 1001 *Western Pathfinder* stands outside the depot. Three months later, it was withdrawn from service and scrapped in 1977.

Left: The 11.05 to Paddington arrives at Westbury from the west on 7 April 2017 with power car 43014 at its head.

Colas Class 70 nos. 70812, 70806 and 70801 leave the stabling point at Westbury coupled together on 7 April 2017.

Class 60 no. 60007 *The Spirit of Tom Kendell* leaves the up yard with a departmental train of ballast on 6 May 2016. The locomotive originally carried the name *Cader Idris*, but was renamed in 2011 after a young engineer who lost his life in an accident.

Today Westbury is a busy rail centre. The yards are always active, particularly the virtual quarry on the up side. Movements between Westbury and Eastleigh yards and vice versa take place daily and there are movements between Westbury and Fairwater yard in Taunton. Other destinations from Westbury are the Midlands and South Wales.

Many of the bulk-loaded stone trains from Whatley and Merehead quarries to Theale, Acton and other destinations come through the station, as do Southampton to South Wales freightliners.

Of the passenger services, some Paddington to West of England line trains stop at Westbury. There is a regular service between Cardiff and Portsmouth, with some variations in destination. There is also a regular service between Bristol and Weymouth and a periodic service between Westbury and Swindon. All these are operated by the revived GWR company.

South Western Railway now operates trains from Waterloo to Bristol. Such services would not have been possible in pre-nationalisation days; the original GWR would not have granted running powers!

Left: Western Class no. D1012 *Western Firebrand* at Fairwood Junction with the 16.30 Paddington to Paignton on 6 July 1974.

Below: Class 59 no. 59002 *Alan J Day* on the goods line at Westbury with a Merehead to Theale stone train on 21 July 2016.

A West of England to Paddington HST passes Westbury Panel Box on 19 April 2013, with 43133 at the rear.

A colourful Class 66 no. 66718 *Sir Peter Hendy CBE* poses during a light engine movement on 06 May 2016.

Top: 153325 backs on to a Bristol service on 7 April 2017.

Above: Class 159 no. 159020 stops at Westbury with a Bristol to Waterloo train on 21 July 2016.

Left: Class 47 no. 47832 joins the Westbury station line at Fairwood Junction with a service for Paddington in 2005.

Chapter 20

Berks & Hants Extension Railway and Devizes Branch

I t may seem odd that this route through Wiltshire should be called the Berks and Hants Extension Railway, when no part of this route falls into Hampshire. In 1845, an Act of Parliament was passed allowing the Great Western Railway to build two lines diverging south of Reading, the first to Basingstoke and the other to Hungerford. Both lines were termed the 'Berks and Hants Railway', with only the Basingstoke line passing into Hampshire. When the railway was extended from Hungerford to Devizes in 1862, 'Extension' was added to the line's name.

The line to Hungerford was the first to be completed in 1847, followed a year later by that to Basingstoke. The lines diverged at Southcote Junction, south-west of Reading. The railway was initially built to broad-gauge standard, the GWR's favoured track gauge, but was converted in 1874. The Berks and Hants Extension Railway was originally conceived as the first part of a direct railway to Exeter, but the GWR was beaten by the LSWR's route via Salisbury.

After Hungerford, the B&HER enters Wiltshire alongside the Kennet and Avon Canal at Froxfield and runs in close association to Wootton Rivers. At Devizes, the line's intended destination, it met the Wilts Somerset & Weymouth Railway branch from Holt Junction, allowing a through route to Westbury.

The first station after the Berks and Hants Extension enters Wiltshire is at Great Bedwyn. The station, opened in 1862, is known as Bedwyn, to serve the two villages of Little and Great

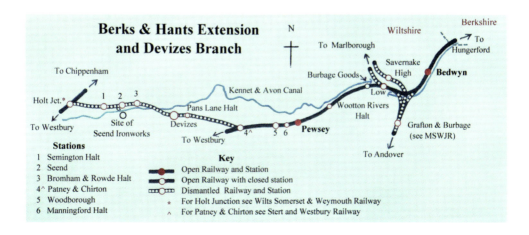

Berks & Hants Extension and Devizes Branch

Stations
1 Semington Halt
2 Seend
3 Bromham & Rowde Halt
4^ Patney & Chirton
5 Woodborough
6 Manningford Halt

Key
Open Railway and Station
Open Railway with closed station
Dismantled Railway and Station
* For Holt Junction see Wilts Somerset & Weymouth Railway
^ For Patney & Chirton see Stert and Westbury Railway

Class 50 no. 50009 *Conqueror* passing Froxfield Bottom Lock with the 14.25 Paddington to Plymouth on 8 July 1980.

Class 50 no. 50020 *Revenge* with the 16.30 Paddington to the West of England at Little Bedwyn on 10 April 1979.

Class 47 no. 47465 races through Great Bedwyn, passing Bedwyn signal box with a Paddington to the West of England express on 2 August 1977.

Class 50 no. 50022 Anson approaches Bedwyn station with the 10.54 Penzance to Paddington on 29 August 1978.

Bedwyn, which are adjacent to one another. Bedwyn is the terminus of outer suburban trains from Reading and Paddington, but prior to the closure of most of the stations on the line towards Devizes and Westbury in the 1960s, other onward services stopped here, primarily to Trowbridge and Westbury. Goods facilities were withdrawn in September 1964.

An up line service calling at Bedwyn, *c*1908. The train is probably from Westbury and either terminates at Reading or Paddington. It is interesting to compare this picture with that taken 70 years later; note that the wooden steps have been taken away and the bridge parapet boarded. The locomotive escapes identity.

Class 50 no. 50039 *Implacable* seen west of Bedwyn with the 16.30 Paddington to the West of England on 16 April 1979.

Class 47 no. 47030 passes Crofton Pumping Station with a relief to the Cornish Riviera on 13 April 1982.

Above: Class 50 no. 50010 *Monarch* at Crofton with the 17.30 Paddington to Plymouth on 16 April 1979.

Right: Class 47 no. 47090 photographed through a catch points warning with loaded stone wagons at Crofton on 29 May 1981.

Below: HST power car 43136 on the rear of a Penzance to Paddington service rounds the sharp curve at Crofton on 28 September 2016. The front power car (out of shot) was no. 43143. The HST units running on the Western Region were originally numbered as sets in the 253 series, but it became difficult to keep the formations together as power cars were taken out of service. It was inevitable that set identification numbers were removed.

At Savernake there was both a High and Low Level station, which is remarkable for such a small place. There was a bay platform at Savernake Low Level station, which was used for a Marlborough shuttle service. In 1947, the GWR operated ten trains a day in each direction, with an extra three each way from High Level. The latter were through trains from Andover to Cheltenham and vice versa. Savernake Low Level closed for goods traffic in May 1964 and to passengers in April 1966. The truncated remains of the branch were in situ in 1976, but in 2017, all that remained were some visible reminders of the branch trackbed where it used to diverge from the main line.

Above: Class 50 no. 50046 *Ajax* passes Savernake Signal Box with a Paddington-bound express on 26 July 1976. Savernake Low Level station was in the immediate foreground of the picture. The truncated remains of the Marlborough branch probably served as a departmental siding at this date.

Left: Savernake Low Level station on 6 July 1959. An MSWJ route train with Swindon-based pannier tank no. 9790 in charge, is shortly to leave the main-line platform and fork right at the junction. A Marlborough train starting at Low Level is seen in the bay opposite. The restricted photographic location has unfortunately obscured the front of the locomotive with semaphore signals.

Class 50 no. 50013 *Agincourt* passes the site of Savernake station on 2 February 1977 with a Paddington to West of England express.

Shortly after Savernake there was, until October 1947, a goods station at Burbage Wharf. It was opened shortly after the Berks and Hants Extension was opened in 1862. Facilities were a goods shed and cattle pens and a signal box to control movements. A station was originally intended, but was built at Savernake, presumably it was a more appropriate site for the branch to Marlborough. Nothing remains and there is no access.

In 1928, the GWR built a small station at Wootton Rivers, called Wootton Rivers Halt. It was a simple affair with platforms made of wooden planks with small corrugated shelters on each platform. In 1947, the all-stations trains to Devizes, Westbury or Trowbridge stopped there, about six in each direction on weekdays. Little had changed by 1955 into British Railways days, but ten years later, the service had been run down and closure took place in 1966.

The next station westward is Pewsey, which is open and still has a main-line train service to Paddington and the West of England. When built it was a single track and platform station, but in preparation for the opening of the Stert and Westbury railway in 1906, it was doubled in 1899. The signal box was removed in 1966 when most of the Berks and Hants stations closed west of Bedwyn.

Left: Wootton Rivers Halt station in 1963.

Below: HST power car 43031 arrives at Pewsey with the 13.21 departure for Paddington on 11 September 2009. The brick-built waiting room is a replacement for an earlier wooden one and is architecturally compatible with the main station building. (SU 161 604)

Above: Manningford Halt, seen in 1964.

Right: Merchant Navy 35028 *Clan Line* coasts through Woodborough with the Venice Simplon Orient Express stock on its way to Bath on 13 June 2016. (SU 107 595)

Opened in 1932, Manningford Halt was very similar in appearance to Wootton Rivers Halt and had the same stopping service. Closure came on the same date in 1966 as the other stations deemed uneconomical on the route. A short distance further, Woodborough station was more substantial, with a goods shed and yard. This also closed in 1966. There are up sidings and goods loops in both directions existing at Woodborough and can be clearly observed from a road overbridge.

Above: HST power car 43079 heads an express to the west at Manningford on 10 March 2012, near the site of a halt closed in 1966. (SU 141 596)

Left: Woodborough station, *c*1908. Note the width of the goods shed entrance, designed for broad gauge and changed to standard gauge in 1874.

Woodborough yard and goods loops seen from an overbridge on 13 June 2012. Class 66 no. 66046 is in the up loop with a loaded stone train from the Somerset quarries, waiting for a Paddington-bound HST with 43177 at its head to pass. (SU 104 596)

Class 50 no. 50043 *Eagle* passes through Woodborough with a West of England express on 29 May 1975.

Beyond Woodborough, after the line was opened in 1862, the next station was at Devizes, where the Berks and Hants met the Wilts, Somerset and Weymouth Railway's branch from Holt Junction opened in 1857. This was the end of the Extension line that enabled trains to reach Bristol and Weymouth. The GWR had taken over the WS&WR in March 1850 and the latter company ceased to exist by an Act of Parliament in July 1851, but I have used the original company name to initially describe the Devizes juncture.

There were, however, two stations subsequently built between Woodborough and Devizes; the first at Patney and Chirton, which was built as part of the Stert and Westbury Railway, a direct line to Westbury avoiding the longer Devizes route. This station became the junction station for the Devizes line, which from July 1900 effectively became a branch line.

The second station was at Pans Lane Halt on the Devizes branch. It was opened as Pans Lane Bridge Halt in 1929, but was soon changed to Pans Lane Halt. The station was built during a spurt of halt building by the Great Western Railway; this example was to serve the nearby Roundway Hospital. It closed along with the rest of the Devizes branch in 1966.

Shortly after joining the Devizes branch from Patney and Chirton, a pick-up goods hauled by an unidentified 61xx tank engine heads towards Devizes. The setting sun of an April day in 1961 picks out the train from the long shadows cast by the trees.

Castle Class no. 5018 *St Mawes Castle* with a Reading to Westbury stopping service passes Stert in June 1962. The Castle was a large engine to be used on this service, but by 1962 diesel had taken hold and, no doubt, there were many spare engines available, albeit not in the best condition.

Right and below: Pans Lane Halt, photographed shortly before closure in 1965. The shiny rails show the line was still being used, but the station is unkempt. The corrugated shelter is typical of a Wiltshire halt built around 1930.

Bottom: A troop special stopped at Devizes on 4 May 1962, hauled by Castle Class no. 7001 *Sir James Milne*. The train originated in the Midlands.

9F 92002 seems to have an escape of steam as it stands with the fireman on the tender at Devizes, c1962. The train is believed to be the 23.30 Hoo Junction to Severn Tunnel Junction cement working.

Devizes train service in 1947 consisted of third-class-only shuttles to Patney and Chirton with Pans Lane Halt as the only intermediate stop. Another third-class-only, all-stations service was to Trowbridge. Through trains ran between Paddington and Westbury or Trowbridge, with a few continuing to Bath and Bristol.

Despite the line being classified as a branch line, it played an important role as a diversionary route in the event of engineering works between Fairwood Junction, west of Westbury, and Patney and Chirton. Furthermore, it could also serve as an alternative route to Bristol.

There were three platforms at Devizes and a goods yard with shed.

Goods facilities were withdrawn in November 1964 and passenger services on 18 April 1966.

The eastern portal of Devizes tunnel seen from the footpath from St. John's churchyard in 2016. (SU 004 612)

Devizes station after closure, *c*1968. The site is now a car park. (SU 002 614)

It is difficult to appreciate that a railway ever existed in Devizes, as the station site is now a large car park. From the east, there was a tunnel under Devizes Castle to reach the station. I believe the western portal is a rifle range, but the eastern portal can be seen from a footpath at the rear of St John's churchyard. Onward from Devizes, the track bed is on an embankment and can be seen from the road to Melksham; the bridge abutments are visible as the line crossed the canal.

Below left and below right: Bromham and Rowde Halt, seen around the time of closure in 1966.

The next station after crossing the canal is Bromham and Rowde Halt. The villages that the station is named after are two miles away down country lanes. The station was opened in 1909 and was staffed – note the porter's cabin at the end of the platform. This suggests the halt was busier than many branch line halts.

Seend station was half a mile away from Bromham and Rowde. The station was opened shortly after the line was built in 1857 and was about one mile from the village centre. There was an iron works at Seend Cleeve and connection was made to the station yard to transport pig iron and coal. The formation bed of the connection can still be seen from above the canal at Seend Cleeve. (ST 932 614)

Left: A Westbury to Reading stopping train arrives at Seend with Castle Class no. 5039 *Rhuddlan Castle* in charge on 18 April 1964.

Below: Seend station in 1908.

Above: Seend seen after closure in 1968.

Right: Semington Halt in 1968 after closure.

Castle Class no. 7021 *Haverfordwest Castle* coming off the Devizes branch at Holt Junction in 1960 with the 4.36pm Newbury to Trowbridge stopper.

Smelting stopped at the site in 1876 and it was abandoned, although quarrying carried on spasmodically up to 1946. The station was enlarged in 1906 with an additional platform for trains to cross.

Seend signal box was closed in 1956 and the line singled, leaving the down platform out of commission. After this, the goods sidings were controlled by a ground frames and electric train token system. The station closed in 1966 and the track was lifted around 1970, when many of the line's buildings were demolished.

The last station before Holt Junction was Semington Halt, which opened in 1906. The wooden platform appears lower than usual and the wooden waiting shelter is not typical of others on the line.

Chapter 21

The Stert and Westbury Railway

D espite the L&SWR beating the GWR to the short route to Exeter, it was still in the interests of the Great Western to create a short cut to the west, rather than take the 'Great Way Round' via Bristol. Furthermore, taking a shorter route to Westbury would also cut the time taken to reach Weymouth. With these goals in mind, the Stert to Westbury line was engineered and a new junction created between Patney and Stert.

A new station on the original Berks and Hants extension was built at Patney, called Patney Bridge. However, this was soon changed to Patney and Chirton, including the village a little to the south of Patney, for reasons of confusion between Patney Bridge and Putney Bridge, a station in London.

Patney and Chirton station originally had three platforms. One of these was an island platform for up trains on the new Westbury route; trains on the Devizes line used the north side of the island. Upon the opening of the direct route to Westbury, the Devizes line was reduced to branch status. A goods yard opened beside the station in 1904. In 1909, another platform was added for military use, separate and north of the other platforms. There was direct access to this from the north side of the main line.

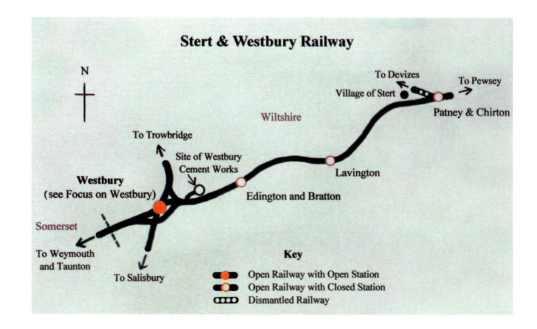

235

Patney and Chirton station, *c*1910.

The route opened in July 1900 and opening of the passenger stations on the line quickly followed. By 1906, the Taunton line had been extended beyond Castle Cary and was open to Taunton. The short cut to the west was complete; Castle Cary became a junction for the Weymouth line.

Patney and Chirton closed to pick-up goods traffic in May 1964 and to passengers in 1966 and was soon demolished, leaving the long footbridge in situ, which today is the only reminder that a station ever existed at this location. Fortunately, the footbridge is a public footpath and the only safe means of crossing the railway.

Above left and above right: Lavington station main building and home signals and signal box, *c*1968.

Below: Class 50 no. 50042 *Triumph* with a Paddington to Plymouth express at Lavington on 5 May 1980.

Class 66 no. 66614 in Freightliner green livery passes an up IET to Paddington at Bratton Road, near Edington, on 25 May 2022.

Lavington station was named after the major communities of Market Lavington and West Lavington, despite being closer to Littleton Panell. The station and goods yard opened when the line opened in 1900. In common with all the intermediate stations between Pewsey and Westbury, it closed in 1966. The goods yard lasted a little longer, closing in March 1967. The station was demolished not long after closure, but the signal box remained for occasional use until 1979. During this time, when unmanned, it would have been switched out, in other words the main line signals would all have shown clear.

The only other station between Patney and Westbury was Edington and Bratton, which opened for goods in July 1900 and for passengers a few weeks later. Its passenger receipts must have been poor because it closed for passengers in November 1952 and the station buildings

Edington and Bratton station *c*1910.

were demolished not long after. The goods yard fared better, but still closed before both Patney and Chirton and Lavington, in March 1963.

Before the line reached Westbury, it passed Westbury Cement Works, with its tall 40ft chimney and effluent trail, which could be seen for miles. The Works was built in the early 1960s and had its own sidings for receipt of coal and despatch of cement. The site was mothballed in 2009 and the chimney demolished in September 2016.

Westbury has had a railway station since the Wilts Somerset and Weymouth Railway from Chippenham terminated there in 1848 and was subsequently extended to Weymouth under the GWR. To accommodate the new line's extension of the Berks and Hants Extension from Stert to Westbury, the station was rebuilt in 1899. Since 1933, an avoiding line has skirted the town and station of Westbury.

Above left: Westbury Cement Works sidings a year or so before closure. An HST from the west passes Westbury Cement Works on 25 March 2015.

Above right: Grange Class no. 6819 *Highnam Grange* comes off Westbury shed on 9 November 1963 to pick up a rake of loaded cement wagons.

Below: Westbury station, *c*1905.

Chapter 22

The Midland and South Western Junction Railway

T he route of the MSWJR meandered through Wiltshire almost north to south. There are two remnants upon which rails still exist, although one section has been replaced in preservation.

At Blunsdon, between Swindon and Cricklade, the Swindon and Cricklade Railway is bringing back to life a section of railway between Cricklade and Mouldon Country Park. In the extreme south of the county, at Ludgershall, the line is still open from Andover to the military base, but operated as a long siding.

Two-thirds of the MSWJR route ran through Wiltshire. It has origins in the 1870s (various schemes were mooted from 1846 onward), to its closure to passenger traffic in September 1961 and to goods in various stages between 1964 and 1970. All the route illustrations are, however, in Wiltshire.

The GWR guarded its territory and tried to disrupt and argue against any north-to-south route involving rival companies that crossed its path. A route from the Midlands to the South Coast was considered as early as 1846, crossing the main broad-gauge line of the GWR at Swindon. Broad gauge gave the GWR a potential advantage in speed and stability over narrow gauge, but the competing companies were all using narrow-gauge track. In an attempt to prevent rival companies building through what it considered its own territory, the GWR dual-gauged its track between Oxford and Basingstoke, effectively providing a through route to the South Coast without having to change trains.

However, it was inevitable that railways connecting the Midlands with the South would continue to be promoted. The initial stages of connecting Cheltenham with Southampton via Swindon and Marlborough started with the promotion of a railway between Swindon and Andover, to be known as the Swindon, Marlborough and Andover Railway (SM&AR).

Mogul 5306 is ready to depart Marlborough for Swindon Town in September 1961.

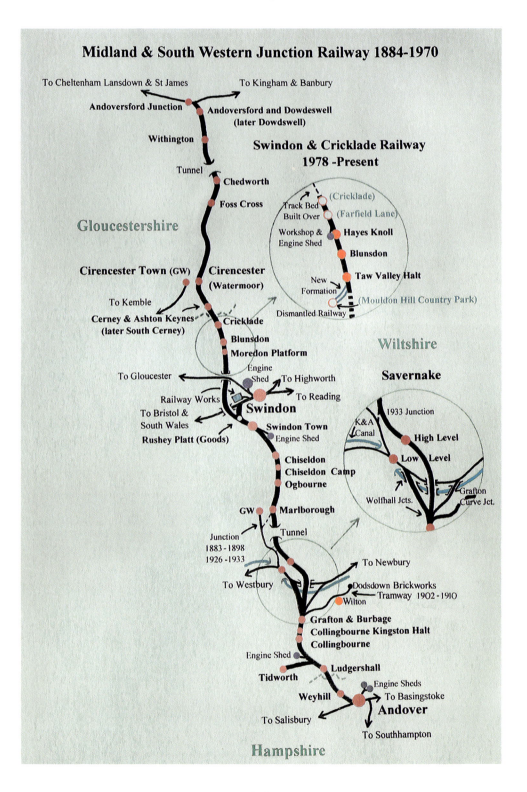

After many setbacks and a change of planned alignment at Swindon to a station in the old town and construction of its own station in Marlborough, the line opened in July 1881. Intermediate stations were built at Chiseldon and Ogbourne. Further advancement was planned via running powers on an already existing branch line from the GWR station at Savernake to its own station at Marlborough. This was steeply graded and required a connecting line from the SM&AR to the GWR track. Furthermore, their trains had to run along the Berks and Hants Extension Railway of the GWR to reach a new junction east of Savernake station at Wolfhall Junction.

The extension south from Wolfhall Junction to Andover had intermediate stations at Grafton and Burbage, Collingbourne, Ludgershall and Weyhill. However, the use of the GWR line and station between Marlborough and Wolfhall Junction was fraught with difficulties. The GWR held trains at signals to give preferential passage to its own services and a ticket inspection at Savernake station caused further delays.

North of Swindon, the Swindon and Cheltenham Extension Railway (S&CER) promoted a line from Rushey Platt to Andoversford, east of Cheltenham, which joined the Banbury and Cheltenham Direct Railway, affiliated to the GWR. At Rushey Platt, it joined the connecting line from the SM&AR old town station to the GWR station. The line initially reached Cirencester, with intermediate stations at Cricklade and Cerney and Ashton Keynes (later shortened to Cerney), and was worked from the start by the SM&AR.

It was inevitable that the resources of the SM&AR and the S&CER would be pooled, and they amalgamated to form the MSWJR in June 1884. The line was open between Cirencester and Red Post Junction on the London and South Western Railway at Andover, but the company fell into financial difficulties and went into receivership. The costly service connecting the Swindon stations operated by the SM&AR was immediately suspended.

5700 Class Pannier no. 8793 at Marlborough Low Level with a passenger service, c1960.

The only way to save the company from winding up was to continue construction north of Cirencester, but finance had to be raised and the creditors satisfied with the course of action proposed; ultimately in part, through issue of debenture stock.

There were setbacks in construction, with a tunnel collapse at Chedworth, problems with access to the GWR line at Andoversford Junction and the readiness of the Midland Railway to accept additional trains into Cheltenham station. Eventually these were resolved and the line opened in August 1891 from the Midland station (Lansdown) to Andover. By 1892, it was possible to travel direct from the Midlands to Southampton with through carriages.

North of Cirencester, there were intermediate stations at Foss Cross, Chedworth, Withington, Dowdeswell and Andoversford Junction. Dowdeswell was renamed Andoversford and Dowdeswell in 1897.

By the end of 1891, the railway was still in receivership. Sam Fay was seconded from the L&SWR to become General Manager, to improve the financial status and wellbeing of the company. Within a short time, he had removed from their duties all the senior officers of the M&SWJR who were deemed responsible for the situation of the company and later, the official receiver, who was a company director of the railway, was contrived out of office and his place taken by Sam Fay. He now held all the reins of manager and receiver and, after successfully increasing receipts, was able to pay off the outstanding creditors and under an Act of 1897 obtained a discharge from receivership.

The gradient on the Great Western line from Marlborough was 1 in 50 in places, which affected the loading of the MSWJR trains using the line to Savernake Great Western station. This, coupled with the delays caused by an awkward GWR over lines on which the M&SWJR had running powers, caused the promotion of a bypass railway from Marlborough to beyond Wolfhall Junction with the Berks and Hants Extension (a name still retained today) to a new

An old postcard c1905, showing both Marlborough stations. In the GWR station are two carriages. The locomotive appears to be running around, with only the steam showing from behind a building. There are a number of coal wagons in the GWR yard.

Marlborough. Showing the G.W.R. Station on the left, and M. & S.W.J. Station on the right.

On the opening of the G.W.R. from Marlborough to Savernake, all the great people of the neighbourhood were on the train, and the event was probably too much for the engine, as it failed in its first effort to climb the incline, and it is related that a dog running alongside, reached Savernake before its master

One of three M&SWJR locomotives still extant in the early 1950s, 1335, is seen on a Stephenson Locomotive Society special working into the Cotswolds from Oxford on 31 August 1952. This locomotive was built in 1894 by Dubs and Co and carried the number 11 under the M&SWJR. All three engines were fitted with Belpaire boilers in 1924 by the GWR and transferred to the Reading District. 1334 was withdrawn from Didcot in 1952 and 1335/6 were withdrawn from Reading in 1952 and 1954 respectively.

junction at Grafton. This would create a continuous M&SWJR route without accessing the GWR in Wiltshire at all.

Proposals were put forward but the initial attempts were thwarted by the GWR, there being an existing, albeit problematic, route operated by the objecting company. However, in 1894, a successful proposal was put forward in collaboration with the 5th Earl of Ailesbury, Henry Brudenell-Bruce, whose land the line would pass over. A bill was placed before Parliament to create a bypass to the GWR at Savernake, for operating reasons to be known as the Marlborough and Grafton Railway. This was a separate company to the existing M&SWJR because the latter company was still in receivership and there was no possibility of such a bill passing acceptance.

The new extension was to be constructed in double-track formation with a tunnel outside Marlborough. This reduced the maximum gradient to 1 in 100, increasing the loading on the M&SWJR trains, and allowed the connections with the GWR at both Marlborough and Wolfhall Junction to be removed, with the line from Wolfhall being retained as a siding. A station was built called Savernake High Level, which included a private waiting room for the Earl of Ailesbury.

By 1897, with the M&SWJR free from the receiver, it absorbed the M&GR in 1899.

A station at Blunsdon was opened in 1895. Rushey Platt closed for passengers in 1905 and a platform was opened at Moredon in 1913, for goods only. Most of the route mileage was doubled between 1900 and 1902, aided by a loan from the Midland Railway.

A very short-lived and little known standard-gauge tramway existed between 1902 and 1910 between Grafton and Burbage station (then known as Grafton) and Dodsdown Brickworks, near Wilton. The two-mile-long line left the M&SWJR a little north of Grafton station and took an easterly course to the north of Wilton village to reach the brickworks. Trains were run under gravity from the brickworks to Grafton station, the bricks being destined for the construction of Tidworth Barracks. Empties were taken back to the brickworks by steam engine. The track was lifted by 1920.

In 1901, a branch to Tidworth from Ludgershall was opened. It was constructed by contractors for the War Office and initially used for military personnel, stores and workmen constructing Tidworth barracks. In 1902, it was opened for general goods and the operation of a public service. The M&SWJR adopted it by leasing it from the War Office in 1903. Ironically not owned by the railway company, it was the most profitable part of the MSWJR system.

In 1905, the GWR secured running powers over the M&SWJR south from the Berks and Hants by installing a junction from east to south, known as the Grafton curve. This was used for military traffic. It closed in 1957.

Collingbourne station, c1960.

Collingbourne Kingston Halt on 4 April 1959.

After all the problematic years of association with the GWR, the grouping of Britain's railways in 1923 saw the M&SWJR absorbed into the GWR, followed in 1924 by the closure of Blunsden station. In the same year, Cerney station was renamed South Cerney. The connection between Marlborough, M&SWJR station and the High Level GWR line reopened in 1926 for wagon movements.

Shortly after the grouping, the passenger service between Swindon Old Town and Junction stations was restored in 1923, no longer incurring running power costs.

Above left: Savernake High Level station on 6 July 1959. Some engineering work is going on, with departmental wagons occupying the southbound line.

Above right: The remains of Savernake High Level station in 2008, seen from the road bridge in the background of the 1959 picture. The platform faces can still be discerned through the undergrowth. (SU 222 642)

The bridge abutments on a lane connecting Wootton Rivers with Cadley, seen in 2008. The foreground bridge was the GWR line to Marlborough and the rear abutments were for the M&SWJR bypass route through HIgh Level station. (SU 213 642)

Above left: **Ludgershall station looking towards Andover in 1928.**

Above right: **The remarkable effect of Tidworth station engraved on a black marble slab, one of a number of such slabs emulating Stonehenge on Tidworth War Memorial.**

The M&SWJR's absorption into the GWR did have the benefit of improved maintenance to the fabric of the line, including strengthening of bridges to allow larger GWR locomotives access to the route.

New station halts were constructed at Chiseldon Camp in December 1930 and at Collingbourne Kingston in April 1932. In 1933, the lines from Savernake to Marlborough were rationalised. The double track of the ex-M&GR bypass was operated as two single lines. The down (southbound) was dedicated to through trains and the up line (northbound) was used by Savernake Low Level to Marlborough trains. This allowed much of the old GWR branch, including High Level station, to be closed, using a link to the northbound track where the two lines ran side by side.

World War Two was an important period for the line, which was selected as a major cross-country supply route between the Midlands and the port of Southampton. It was anticipated that the expected German onslaught by the Luftwaffe would sever most of the rail network in the London area. In the event, this did not materialise. The Battle of Britain, fought in the skies over Britain, ultimately foiled the German invasion scenario. Nevertheless, the old M&SWJR route was considered a short cut from Southampton to points north from Cheltenham.

Additional traffic was generated during the conflict on the Tidworth branch and, of course, in the Salisbury Plain and Marlborough Downs area, where there was much preparation for D-Day involving military training and campsites. Savernake Forest was used for storing vast amounts of ammunition in purpose-built shelters.

To the advantage of the rail line, the war had brought improvements to the operating capability of the line through long passing loops to accommodate lengthy freight trains and better signalling to cope with an increase in traffic. Unfortunately for rail, road traffic was becoming more cost-effective.

On 1 January 1948, Britain's railways passed into public ownership. The M&SWJR was split between the Western Region and Southern Region just north of Grafton station. The Western had control of the track from Grafton northward and the Southern from Grafton station to the south. In 1958, a further regional reorganisation brought the whole line under Western Region control.

With regard to the locomotive stock: The M&SWJR had its own locomotive fleet. The earliest engines were purchased by the S,M&AR between 1881 and 1884; all were tanks. Following its foundation, the M&SWJR purchased 11 locomotives from 1893 to 1898 of varying wheel arrangements. Subsequent to 1899, there was a degree of standardisation and a further 19 engines were ordered, all with wheel arrangements of either 0-6-0 or 4-4-0 tender types.

Ogbourne station c1960.

All the company's locomotives were withdrawn before nationalisation, with the exception of three 2-4-0 engines, which were numbered 1334–1336 by the GWR. The last of these, 1336, was withdrawn from service in 1954. Their light weight made them useful to the GWR for branch line work away from the M&SWJR.

There were locomotive sheds housing M&SWJR engines at Cheltenham, Swindon Town, Ludgershall and Andover Junction.

Post-1923, Great Western locomotives also worked the line. 'Duke' class and 43xx Moguls were commonplace. Pannier tanks dominated the shuttle service, certainly after nationalisation. Through trains were sometimes worked by 'Manors'.

My own reflections of the line centre on a loco-spotters' special operated by Ian Allan on 10 April 1958. I picked the special up at Reading with a friend for a run behind 3440 *City of Truro* and Mogul 6316. After a visit to Swindon Locomotive Works, we were taken down the connecting line past Rushey Platt to pick up the old M&SWJR route through Swindon Town to Andover, then onwards to visit Eastleigh Works – unforgettable!

I also recall a spell of observation at Lansdown Junction in Cheltenham in the hope of seeing traffic come off the M&SWJR from the Andoversford link. Sometimes 'U' class Southern locomotives were used. On the day of observation, I saw 31618 on a through service from Andover in the early afternoon. If it was the same train as in my copy of the 1955 timetable, there were through coaches from Southampton and the service left Andover station at 11.07 in the morning.

The principal freight traffic on the line under M&SWJR ownership was coal from the Welsh and Forest of Dean coalfields, which travelled over the junction with the GWR at Rushey Platt, heading south to destinations on the L&SWR. It is well known that Reading, on the GWR, was known for beer, biscuits and bulbs – on the M&SWJR, it was Burton beer and Bristol bricks. Then, of course, the ubiquitous pick-up goods and the significant military traffic should not be forgotten. Military traffic continued to use the line after the grouping in 1923 and nationalisation in 1948.

Notwithstanding the early years of securing sufficient and adequate passenger stock through financial difficulty, at its best in the latter years of operating a passenger service on the M&SWJR, there were trains with through carriages from Manchester, Birmingham and Derby to Southampton

and a good service between Swindon Town and Southampton. In the 1950s, when the line was being run down through lack of passenger receipts, only one through train a day ran each way.

In 1955, the Tidworth passenger service ceased and operation of the line was transferred back to the War Department. The railway was no longer promoted as a through route from the Midlands to Southampton, there being a much faster and well-used service through Oxford to reach the coastal ports and resorts of Hampshire and Dorset. The railway was in severe decline and in 1958 Savernake High Level was closed because, it was said, the bridges over the canal and main line required attention. In the event, this hastened the closure of the bypass line through Savernake and the track was lifted in 1960. The remaining services ran through Savernake Low Level, but the old M&SWJR line was losing a substantial amount of money and passenger trains over the whole route between Cheltenham and Andover were withdrawn in September 1961.

Freight continued for a few years on isolated sections of the route. Savernake to Marlborough goods traffic ceased in 1964, as did freight to Cirencester from Swindon Town. The power station at Moredon continued to receive coal by train until 1969. This service required reversal at Rushey Platt after leaving the main line through Swindon. Swindon Town continued to be used for stone traffic during construction of the M4 until the end of 1970.

Track over the route was mostly lifted by 1978, but the route through Wiltshire is clearly visible from Collingbourne towards Burbage while on the A338, and from Ogbourne to Chiseldon on the A346. There are remains of bridge abutments over the Kennet and Avon

Above: A bridge over a lane at Collingbourne carries the old M&SWJR track bed. (SU 242 551)

Below left: The remains of a platform at Rushey Platt, Swindon. (SU 133 837)

Below right: The footpath and cycleway looking south from Chiseldon on the M&SWJR track bed. (SU 193 793)

Canal above Crofton Top Lock and many other bridge remains as the route crosses Wiltshire, but the M4 has destroyed most of the route evidence immediately south of Swindon. Some of the track mileage has been retained as a footpath and cycleway, notably in Swindon, Chiseldon and Marlborough. North of Swindon, some route mileage has been preserved in the name of The Swindon and Cricklade Railway.

In 1978, a public meeting was held to determine the interest and feasibility of recreating part of the M&SWJR between Swindon and Cricklade. A year later, the volunteer organisation of the Swindon and Cricklade Railway took over the dismantled track bed from British Rail with the task of recreating a working railway.

In 1983, the line's first working steam engine was delivered, an Andrew Barclay 0-4-0 saddle tank *Richard Trevithick*. By 1985, the collection had increased to six steam engines, four diesels and eight carriages, with much restoration work pending. Following the granting of a light

Above: Swindon Town station, *c*1908 from an old Edwardian postcard. The locomotive is difficult to identify.

Right: The 10.00 train from Cheltenham to Southampton makes its Swindon Town stop with Manor 4-6-0 7810 *Draycott Manor* in charge on 14 June 1957. Some of these through services were hauled by Southern Moguls.

railway order in 1983, the organisation was able to operate a passenger shuttle over half a mile to the north of a small station restored at Blunsdon.

As the track was reinstated northwards toward Cricklade, a new station and locomotive maintenance and running shed have been built at Hayes Knoll. This was an empty site with no road access and was named after a local landscape feature. The name suggests the grandeur of a much bigger station than there really is.

The railway has been extended to South Meadow Lane and beyond (no vehicular access) under phase 1. Phases 2 and 3 are extending to a new halt at Farfield and phase 4 will take track into the outskirts of Cricklade. The terminus at Cricklade will need to be short of the original station, as the old formation has been built over. Further progress depends upon funds and the sourcing of raw materials. This is ongoing, though there is now enough rail secured to reach the destination, while the sourcing of sleepers and purchase of ballast has been a priority.

South of Blunsdon, which is presently the railway's main visitor centre, the line extends to a new station called Taw Valley Halt. This gives a running line more than two miles long. Southwest of the halt is Mouldon Country Park, and there is an intention of creating a southern terminus for the line in the park. The track bed is in place, but all the buildings, rails and facilities are yet to be created. This is a major task, but upon completion, the railway will form a major attraction within the park and, hopefully, significantly boost passenger receipts.

At Hayes Knoll, a Great Western Modified Hall, 6984 *Owsden Hall*, is under restoration and the shed houses Class 73 electro-diesel no. E6003 *Sir Herbert Walker*, which is operational. There are a number of main-line diesel shunters, together with industrial and diesel locomotives in various stages of preservation, some operational.

The railway also has a two-car 'Thumper' diesel-electric unit numbered 1302. In May 2016, however, it was almost completely destroyed by fire. A replacement car for the most severely damaged vehicle will bring it back to life.

Above: In the early years of preservation at Blunsdon in 1982, 56xx tank 5637 and Modified Hall 7903 *Foremarke Hall* are being protected against further corrosion, before full restoration. Neither engine is presently on the line, but both are fully restored.

Left: The restored Blunsdon station, looking south. (SU 109 898)

Above: 3135 *Spartan* with a passenger train at Hayes Knoll station in 2017. The locomotive is an 0-6-0 tank built by Fablok and Co of Poland in 1953 and is owned by the railway.

Right: Hayes Knoll station has an impressive platform frontage, which hides the maintenance and locomotive facilities to its rear. There is no public access to the station, except by means of alighting from a train.

Below left: A new formation veers right from the old M&SWJR track bed into Mouldon Country Park. (SU 119 878)

Below right: The site of a prospective terminus for the Swindon and Cricklade Railway in Mouldon Country Park, photographed in 2017. (SU 128 878)

Chapter 23

London & South Western – Salisbury Direct and Salisbury & Yeovil Railways

lthough Salisbury was reached as early as 1847, it was via Bishopstoke (Eastleigh) on the L&SWR main line to Southampton. This route was by no means direct and, as extensions west from Salisbury to the West Country were considered, it was clearly advisable to establish a more direct route into the city.

Work had started on the Salisbury Direct in 1848, but was halted due to indecision regarding the most appropriate route for the L&SWR to reach Exeter. Furthermore, the GWR was putting proposals forward that trespassed over L&SWR- claimed territory and raised objections to L&SWR proposals to reach Exeter. Pressure was also being exerted from the populace of Andover for a rail connection, being fearful that the halt in construction would take the railway on a different route. Perhaps Exeter would best be reached via Dorchester, which would merely extend the line already present through Southampton.

However, the die was cast when an Act of Parliament was passed allowing a Salisbury to Yeovil railway to be built by a nominally independent company. This authorisation in August 1854 reinvigorated the Salisbury Direct, because the L&SWR had undertaken to extend from

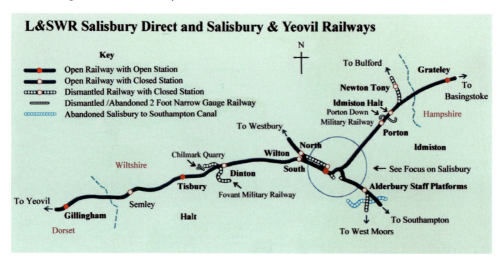

Warship no. D801 *Vanguard* near Idmiston Halt with the 09.00 Waterloo to Exeter on 21 April 1967.

Yeovil to reach Exeter as part of the scenario. The direct line to Salisbury left the Southampton main line at Worting Junction, west of Basingstoke, and travelled via Andover to reach Salisbury (Milford). Initially the line opened to Andover in July 1854, but it took another three years to reach the terminus at Milford.

The initial stage of reaching Exeter was to connect Yeovil with Salisbury. Clearly it would be ill advised to require reversal in Milford for onward westbound traffic. The Salisbury and Yeovil Railway station was at Fisherton in Salisbury (*see* Salisbury in Focus). It was decided that the best option for the L&SWR would be to use Fisherton station via a 443-yard tunnel constructed to connect the Salisbury Direct with the Salisbury and Yeovil Railway, effectively making this a through station. Fisherton opened on 1 May 1859 and from that date passenger trains ceased to use Milford.

Idmiston Halt on 23 April 1967.

PORTON

HE STATION, PORTON

Porton station, from an old Edwardian postcard dated c1910.

The Act of Parliament sanctioning the Salisbury and Yeovil Railway was supported by the L&SWR, which agreed to operate the trains and take up shares in the company. In return, the L&SWR would receive 42.5 per cent of the receipts. Salisbury to Gillingham opened on 1 May 1859 on the same date Salisbury Fisherton station opened. The line was extended to Sherborne on 7 May 1860 and to Yeovil in June.

The line was most successful, as it was a bridge between the L&SWR from Waterloo to Salisbury and onward from Yeovil to Exeter. The shareholders received a lucrative return when the line was sold to the L&SWR in 1878.

Another view of Porton station looking towards Salisbury, taken on 21 April 1967.

S15 no. 30839 at Porton with the 14.47 Salisbury to Waterloo service on 14 July 1962.

Leaving Salisbury near Bishopdown is Class 50 no. 50007 *Sir Edward Elgar* with an Exeter to Waterloo service on 6 June 1987.

Initially, most of the railway from Basingstoke to Yeovil was single track, but it was doubled all the way to Exeter in 1870.

There were two routes to reach Exeter from London: the GWR broad gauge via Bristol and the L&SWR via Salisbury. The Salisbury route was the shortest, with the GWR's other 'Great Way Round' not being shortened until the Berks and Hants' extension to Taunton from Castle Cary was fully opened in 1906. The latter became the preferred route into Devon and Cornwall, travelling alongside the south Devon resorts into Plymouth, across the Tamar by Brunel's famous bridge and along the southern side of Cornwall to Penzance. In contrast, the L&SWR route to Devon and Cornwall after Exeter was circuitous via a number of branch lines, eventually reaching Plymouth by the back door, but still only five miles longer than the GWR.

When Beeching started rationalising lines and closing stations, it was inevitable that the L&SWR route to Exeter would become a secondary status railway, not being closed, however, because it passed through communities with no other rail connections.

Stations on the route started to close in 1966 and the line west of Salisbury was singled in 1967. The long summer Saturday holiday express trains stopping at Sidmouth and Seaton Junctions for the South Devon resorts and often reinforced by extra trains, were no more.

However, there continued to be a through service between Waterloo and Exeter, via Salisbury, at first operated by Western region diesel-hydraulics, followed by Classes 33, 47 and 50 haulage.

Today, the line is operated by Class 159 multiple-units and some parts of the route are being upgraded to meet improving passenger numbers.

The stations on the Salisbury Direct from Worting Junction to Salisbury within Wiltshire are closed with no trace remaining. Overton, Whitchurch and Andover in Hampshire, all opened in July 1854 and remain open, but Oakley, opened at the same time, closed in June 1963. Hurstbourne, situated between Whitchurch and Andover, didn't open until the line was well established in December 1882, and closed in April 1964. Grateley, the last station in

West Country no. 34030 *Watersmeet* with a Brighton to Plymouth train waiting for signals at Salisbury on 10 October 1963.

Hampshire before the county boundary with Wiltshire, opened in May 1857, when the line opened to Milford and remains operational.

The only two stations in Wiltshire before Salisbury were Porton and Idmiston Halt. Porton opened with the section of line between Andover and Salisbury in 1857. Here there was a 2ft narrow-gauge military railway operating from the goods yard to Porton Down Military Camp, one mile to the south-east. It was built in 1916 to transport materials and munitions into the camp, arriving into Porton goods yard by rail. It remained in situ until 1946. Porton goods yard closed in 1962 and the station in 1968.

60163 *Tornado* emulating times past with 'The Devon Belle', working hard at Skew Bridge, between Salisbury and Wilton, on 2 April 2016. (SU 125 307)

Idmiston Halt, which was closer to Porton Down Military Camp than Porton, opened in 1943. Clearly this station must have been used for troop movement by rail in preference to Porton, but the narrow gauge may still have been used for goods of varying nature during the war.

Upon opening of the line to Yeovil, trains ran parallel out of Salisbury with the Great Western line to Westbury, separating east of Wilton, where there was a station on each of the routes. Both were named Wilton until 1949, when the Yeovil line station became Wilton South and the old GWR station became Wilton North. Wilton South closed in 1966 and the goods yard two years earlier.

Prestige expresses such as the 'Devon Belle' that were not booked to stop at Salisbury changed engines at Wilton South to save congestion in the city station. This resulted in the necessity of light engine movements between Salisbury locomotive shed and Wilton station. Wilton South

Above: **Class 37 no. 37710 brings a rake of empty fuel tanks into Salisbury at Skew Bridge, *c*2002.**

Left: **West Country locomotives were often affectionately called 'Spam Cans' for obvious reasons. Here 34038 *Lynton* was photographed at Wilton with a West of England express on 3 May 1963.**

wasn't a timetabled stop, so passengers could not board or alight there. Unlike other regional main lines, there were no water troughs south and west from Waterloo.

Six miles further to the west was Dinton station, which opened with the line in 1859. During World War One, there were many military camps in the vicinity. South of Dinton lies Fovant, which was among the areas in the locality selected for such a camp. The camps were established to prepare the soldiers for trench warfare in France and Belgium.

West Country Pacific no. 34004 *Yeovil* eases the up Atlantic Coast Express (without headboard) through Wilton South station, *c*1960.

Dinton station, *c*1910.

Dinton station after closure, *c*1970.

A scene at Fovant on the Fovant Military Railway from an old postcard dated *c*1916. It was probably taken at the platform constructed at the end of the line opposite the Fovant chalk military badges.

Tisbury station, *c*1915. (Courtesy of Wilts and Swindon History Centre)

In 1915, the Fovant camp had grown sufficiently in size to warrant a railway line to service troop movements and handle munitions and stores to the camp. A branch from Dinton station was built on the down side via a trailing point. At Fovant, a platform was erected near the A30, opposite the hill now containing the Fovant chalk badges. The line was closed after the war, but reopened in 1921 until February 1924 to clear the camps. The track was lifted in 1926, leaving a few landscape features by which to remember the line.

The station was closed in 1966 and the goods yard a year later, but several sidings and the old up line were retained for MoD use to Chilmark. Also at Chilmark were narrow-gauge lines serving Chilmark Quarry, from which the stone to build Salisbury Cathedral was extracted. There is no public access to any of the sites at Chilmark. The lines were taken out of use in 1994 and mostly removed.

Semley station after closure, *c*1968. Note that the down platform is being dismantled.

Tisbury station opened with the line in 1859 and goods facilities followed a year later. The station had a passing loop until the whole line was doubled. When the line was singled in 1967, the passing loop was removed, but in 1986 it was reinstated east of the station.

Semley was the last station in Wiltshire; it also opened in 1859 and closed in March 1966. Some buildings remain in industrial ownership. Over the county boundary in Dorset is Gillingham station, which is still open.

West Country no. 34002 *Salisbury* heads west with a rake of empty milk tanks near Semley in 1964.

Semley station, *c*1910.

Chapter 24

Amesbury and Military Light Railway

In 1882, a scheme was proposed by the London and South Western Railway for a railway line on its route between Basingstoke and Salisbury to Westbury. The line was proposed to run via Shrewton and Amesbury, then to Bristol with an option to seek running powers over the North Somerset Railway or the Somerset and Dorset. Rivalry, once again between the GWR and L&SWR, over territory creep created serious opposition from the former. The GWR's bitter opposition caused the bill to fail in 1883.

In the same year, the GWR proposed a line from Pewsey to Southampton via Salisbury. This was naturally opposed by the L&SWR, as Southampton was deep inside its territory. Despite approval for the line as far as Salisbury, it was never built.

By 1895, Amesbury still had no rail connection and another scheme put forward by the M&SWJR to reach Amesbury from Ludgershall via Bulford was rejected by the Light Railway Commission as being too close to existing or sanctioned stations.

Another scheme by the GWR proposed a light railway between Bemerton, near Salisbury, and Pewsey on the Berks and Hants Extension Railway. The route was via Amesbury and the Avon valley and, despite approval in 1898, it fell on stony ground, as the proposed railway ran over four miles of military land. Unfortunately for the GWR, the L&SWR saw favour with the

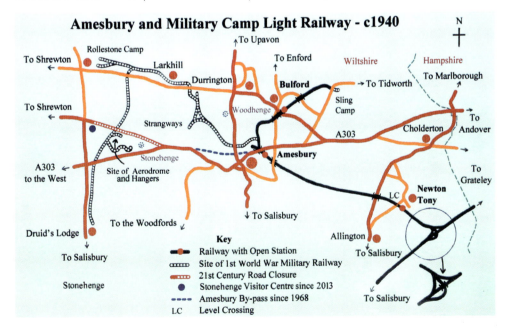

Amesbury and Military Camp Light Railway - c1940

Key
- ●━● Railway with Open Station
- ▭▭▭ Site of 1st World War Military Railway
- ●▭▭● 21st Century Road Closure
- ● Stonehenge Visitor Centre since 2013
- – – – Amesbury By-pass since 1968
- LC Level Crossing

military and consequently became the preferred company to run a railway into Amesbury, which could connect with the Salisbury Plain military facilities.

A light railway order was granted on 24 September 1898, which gave the L&SWR powers to build a railway between a point west of Grateley, near the village of Newton Tony on its 1857 line to Salisbury, to Amesbury and Shrewton. The railway terminated at Amesbury but, for reasons unknown, the line was never extended to Shrewton. However, in 1903, an extension to the line was granted to Bulford and subsequently into the military camp.

Passenger trains started on the Amesbury branch on 2 June 1902, a few months after a goods service was introduced. There was an intermediate station at Newton Tony, but in reality, it was near the start of the branch with the main line. The Bulford extension didn't open until 1 June 1906. Prior to this, in 1904, a connecting curve burrowing under the L&SWR main line at the junction was introduced to avoid crossing the path of up trains between Salisbury and Basingstoke. After the Bulford extension opened, passenger trains ran between there and Salisbury.

Passenger services on the line came to a halt in June 1952, but part of the sanction to extend the line to Bulford was to retain a facility for both passengers and goods at Bulford. I assume this was in relation to the possible need for troop trains and the movement of MoD stores. All goods traffic was withdrawn in March 1963.

There was a station platform within the camp at Bulford, only used for military personnel. There was an exception in its later years when enthusiast specials visited the branch.

The railway into the military camp was extended into Sling Camp, where the New Zealanders were billeted in World War One. Evidence of their stay is cut into the chalk hillside above the camp in the form of a chalk white Kiwi. It is difficult to see from Bulford, however, as trees have obscured the view. The extension into the camp was removed by 1933.

Newton Tony station in 1908.

Amesbury station in 1908.

Although the line wasn't extended to Shrewton, an extensive and lengthy trackwork was installed early in World War One from Amesbury at Ratfyn Junction to serve the camps at Larkhill, Rollestone and down as far as Druid's Lodge on the Salisbury Road. It was operated by the Railway Operating Division of the Royal Engineers. By 1923, it was dismantled and there is nothing to see today, except a large water tower at Druid's Lodge, which may be connected with the military railway.

Amesbury track layout and station in 1955, seen from the road bridge in the background of the 1908 station view.

An Amesbury to Bulford freight stands in Amesbury station on 12 October 1960.

The same train seen from the front with N Class 2-6-0 no. 31810 in charge.

Above: Bulford station, *c*1910.

Right: A home signal preserved at Bulford, 2014.

Chapter 25

Focus on Salisbury

A railway to Salisbury was first mooted in 1837, when an independent company promoted the South Western Railway, and proposed a branch from the London to Southampton line near Basingstoke to Yeovil and Taunton. Salisbury would have been approached via West Dean and a short tunnel to reach the city. A shorter and cheaper alternative proposal left the London to Southampton line at Kingsworthy to reach Salisbury.

In 1838, another scheme was planned to leave the London to Southampton line at Kingsworthy, known as the London and Salisbury Junction Railway. None of these schemes reached fruition.

The first railway to reach Salisbury was a branch from the L&SWR from Bishopstoke (Eastleigh). The line was sanctioned in 1844 and opened in 1847. The terminus was on the eastern outskirts of the city at Milford (see The Bishopstoke to Salisbury Railway). As a passenger station, the terminus was a relatively short-lived location, as the Salisbury Direct Railway was, in 12 years, to join with the Salisbury and Yeovil Railway via a tunnel to reach its station at Fisherton, north-west of the city centre (see the L&SWR Salisbury Direct and Salisbury & Yeovil Railways). This station only had a single platform with a bay. Milford remained open for goods traffic until closure in 1967. There are no physical remains at the Milford site, just an access road and the public house on the corner of the road junction.

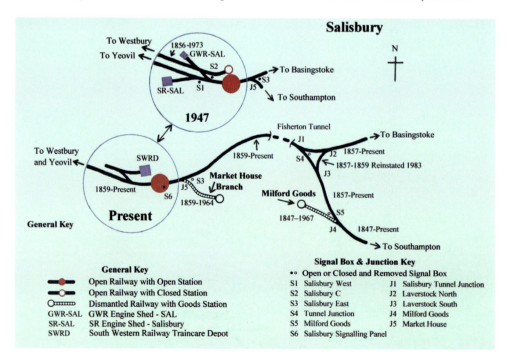

Above left: The original Salisbury & Yeovil/L&SWR station building at Fisherton, Salisbury. (SU 137 301)

Above right: The entrance to Milford Goods adjacent to The Dust Hole public house, also known as The Railway. There are no remains of the goods yard. (SU 152 296)

Below: Milford Goods, 1881. Note the locomotive shed and turntable. (Courtesy Wiltshire and Swindon History Centre)

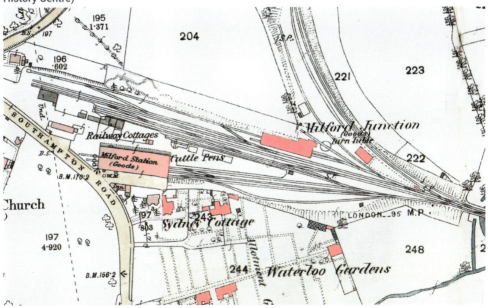

The Great Western Railway station at Fisherton was opened in 1856 as an extension to the Wilts, Somerset & Weymouth Railway. It had two platforms and goods facilities. The station frontage is still in existence as offices and a Railway Staff Club. Little else remains except a water tower and a short length of covered platform. The remainder is a car park, while most of the old Great Western site is taken up with a modern train depot.

The Great Western line was broad gauge, running side by side with the L&SWR as far as Quidhampton, east of Wilton. A transfer shed was built between the GWR and L&SWR to enable goods to be transferred from broad-gauge wagons to the L&SWR standard-gauge

Standard Class 4 no. 76067 approaches Salisbury Tunnel Junction from the Romsey line with a mixed train in 1964.

vehicles. This was an extreme inconvenience, resulting in the broad gauge being converted to standard in 1874. At a later date, connection was made between the two systems, allowing through trains to run into the L&SWR from the GWR onward to the south coast and vice versa. The GWR station closed in 1932 but remained open as a goods depot until 1991. From 1932, all passenger trains used the L&SWR station, which at that time was under Southern Railway control.

Class 158 no. 158888 enters Fisherton Tunnel with a Romsey to Salisbury service on 15 May 2018. (SU 152 310) This was the site of a collision on 31 October 2021, caused by slippage under locked brakes.

A Bulldog class 4-4-0 stands in the Great Western station at Fisherton, *c*1930. (Courtesy of Wilts and Swindon History Centre)

The frontage and remaining structures of the Great Western station, seen from the bay platform at the eastern end of Salisbury's present South Western station. (SU 138 302)

Originally there was a small locomotive depot next to the station, but this was closed when the L&SWR station was enlarged. It was relocated to a site a little further to the west and north of the GWR track and opened in 1899. The depot had a coding of SAL in GWR days and operated as a sub-shed of its home depot of Westbury (WES). It closed in November 1950 under the coding 82D (sub shed), after which date Western engines used the Southern locomotive shed facilities at Salisbury.

The general map of Salisbury railways shows the status of the railways in Salisbury at present and in 1947, shortly before nationalisation. At that time, the GWR shed had an allocation of three locomotives, a pannier tank and two Hall class locomotives. The Great Western line had its own signal box called Westbury C.

In 1973, the four-track arrangement out of Salisbury as far as Quidhampton was rationalised and a connection placed from the Great Western route east of Wilton to join the South Western

Hall Class no. 6955 *Lydcott Hall* comes off the western line from Westbury, passing the GWR signal box, and is about to enter Salisbury station with a freight for the Southampton line, *c*1962.

route. The former GWR double track from there to Salisbury was taken up and all trains now use the South Western lines. A connection was retained at the Quidhampton chalk quarry sidings using a short stretch of the former GWR line, which is no longer used.

I remember there was a daily train in and out of the quarry. This ran from the quarry to Eastleigh yard and was composed of about four or five silver bullet Nacco tankers.

South of and adjacent to the Great Western station was the 1859 stone-built station of the Salisbury and Yeovil / L&SWR. The frontage of this station still exists, which stands in contrast to the brick-built and much larger remodelled layout and station building adjacent, and opened in 1902. Prior to this date, from 1870, the up and down platform faces were staggered. The down platform is in its original location, and the up platform is beyond the present bridge over Fisherton Street.

After 1902, this part of the station was demolished and the site was converted to a marshalling yard, but today, little remains to tell of its former use.

The Great Western engine shed at Salisbury, with an ROD 2-8-0 in prominence. At the time the photograph was taken, *c*1938, it was likely that Westbury had a small number of the class allocated for freight duties. The Railway Operating Division sold 100 of these engines to the GWR between 1919 and 1925. The last survivor then operating on the Western Region was withdrawn in 1958.

Star class no. 4041 *Prince of Wales* at Salisbury with a cross-country from Portsmouth to Cardiff in 1950.

Immediately east of the station, after the Fisherton Street bridge, a branch dropped down to Salisbury Market, built for the opening of the Salisbury to Yeovil line and the L&SWR direct route into Fisherton station.

The line was initiated in 1856, when an Act of Parliament was secured incorporating the Salisbury Railway and Market House Company. The act enabled the construction of a quarter-mile line from the L&SWR immediately east of the Salisbury & Yeovil/L&SWR station to the Market House and various warehouses and maltings.

The railway was leased from the L&SWR at £225 per annum and continued to be leased by the Southern Railway following nationalisation by the British Transport Commission. The line closed in 1964, after the last ten-year lease expired. Subsequently, the tracks were removed, with the area transformed into the Maltings shopping area and an extended car park. The old

Battle of Britain no. 34054 *Lord Beaverbrook* approaches the station with the 11.45 Waterloo to Exmouth and Sidmouth on 14 July 1962.

Market House location is now the Salisbury Public Library. The bridge across the river and a walkway beside the library still exists, leading to the central Market Place.

The L&SWR's original locomotive shed was at Milford. When the new L&SWR station opened in 1859 a locomotive shed was built just west of, and on the south side of, the station. This was only a three-road depot and soon became unfit for purpose.

A much larger depot was constructed further west, again on the south side of the line. This was a ten-road straight shed opened in 1901. By 1950, 57 locomotives were allocated, ranging from 0-4-4 tanks to the mighty Merchant Navy Pacifics. After nationalisation in 1948, locomotive sheds used an alpha-numeric identification coding system. Salisbury became 72B and, after 1962 was known as 70E until closure in 1967.

Since there were no water troughs on the Waterloo to Exeter line, it was quicker to change locomotives at Salisbury on long-distance expresses, or in some cases at Wilton South, rather than spend time filling up the tender tank from the end of platform water columns.

The Great Western site was redeveloped and a new depot opened in 1992 to service the diesel multiple-units now operated by South Western Railway. The original station building designed by Brunel is Grade II listed.

The train services using the station are South Western multiple-units operating between Waterloo and Exeter, with a smattering of Bristol and Yeovil via Westbury services mixed in. Great Western operates trains on the Wessex line between Portsmouth and Cardiff, with additional destinations for some services. Freight consists of stone from the Somerset quarries, departmentals between Westbury and Eastleigh, some MoD traffic and a few freightliners. The Wessex route is also used as a diversion when the line between Southampton and Basingstoke or Basingstoke to Reading is closed.

Salisbury is also a destination for the 'Cathedrals Express' excursions and as such has regular visits of restored steam engines.

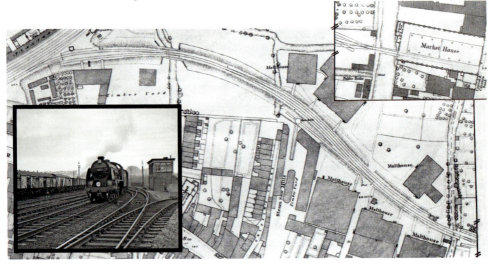

Adapted from a scale 1:500 map dated 1880 of the Salisbury Market House Railway. The Market House is inset in the top right-hand corner of the map. (Courtesy of Salisbury Reference Library)

Inset: A westbound goods approaches Salisbury station with S15 no. 30837 in charge. Dropping to the right is the branch entrance to the Market House Railway.

Salisbury station main entrance, *c*1904, after remodelling. Note the transport of the day. The station forecourt and car park are being remodelled and modernised in 2024.

A pair of T9 4-4-0s 30706 and 30721 have brought into the down bay a train from Bournemouth West, which joined the Romsey line at Alderbury Junction.

A serious accident occurred on 1 July 1906 when an L&SWR boat train from Plymouth to Waterloo derailed at speed, on the sharp curve at the eastern end of Salisbury station. The train ploughed into a milk train and a light engine, killing 28 people.

There was rivalry at the time between the GWR and L&SWR as to which train could reach London first, the GWR with the mail or the L&SWR with passengers. Subsequent to the crash, all trains stopped at Salisbury for many years and a speed restriction of 15mph was imposed.

Left and below: Salisbury shed with King Arthur no. 30449 *Sir Torre* in 1955 and N Class no. 31810 on 17 July 1962.

Bottom: The Atlantic Coast Express with no. 35013 *Blue Funnel* blows off steam as she waits to depart Salisbury for Waterloo in 1960.

Class 66 no. 66097 passes Salisbury Traincare refuelling point with chalk slurry tanks to Eastleigh on 7 February 2007. (SU 135 302)

The train disaster of 1906.

Chapter 26

The Bishopstoke to Salisbury and Salisbury & Dorset Junction Railways

ostilities between the L&SWR and GWR broadly ended on 16 January 1845 after signing an agreement to end territorial battles. However, both companies still protected their own patches rigorously after this date.

In July, the Wilts, Somerset and Weymouth Railway (WS&WR), supported by the GWR, proposed an extension to its already approved line into Salisbury as far as Southampton via Downton and Redbridge. It was never progressed to approval stage.

It was inevitable that a connection to Southampton from Salisbury would be made. Already in the construction stage at the time of the WS&WR proposal was the 1844-approved LSWR

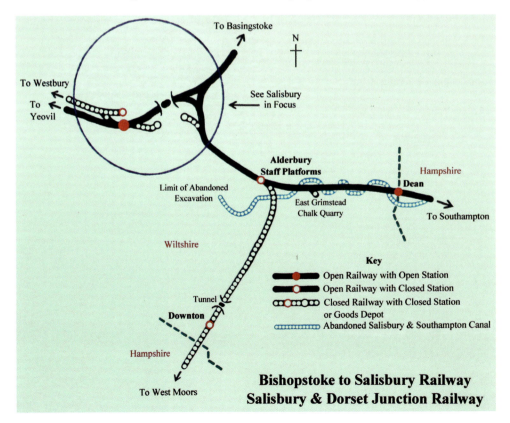

Bishopstoke to Salisbury Railway
Salisbury & Dorset Junction Railway

Above: 60103 *Flying Scotsman* rushes through Dean with a return Cathedrals Express in May 2016 on the Salisbury and Dorset Junction route. The ballast had just been relaid and air turbulence in front of the locomotive has thrown up debris from the ballast. (SU 257 271)

Right: Standard Class 5 no. 73017 arrives at Salisbury with a Brighton to Cardiff service on 10 October 1963.

branch from Bishopstoke (Eastleigh) to Salisbury from the L&SWR main line to Southampton. This was opened to a terminus at Milford on the south side of the city for goods on 27 January 1847 and on 1 March for passengers.

Reaching Salisbury by this route was circuitous and in 1848 a more direct route via Andover was approved. This was opened in 1857 and for two years trains still used the Milford terminus, but a new station in Salisbury at Fisherton, immediately south of the GWR station, was built and opened in 1859.

The only open station in Wiltshire, after Salisbury, on this line is at Dean. The county boundary with Hampshire runs through the eastern end of the station. The other stations on the line after Dean are Mottisfont and Dunbridge (originally Dunbridge), Romsey and Nursling. Nursling was opened in 1882 and closed in 1957. The ex L&SWR main line to Southampton and Weymouth is joined at Redbridge.

The original route to Bishopstoke (Eastleigh) is now a branch from the Wessex main line at Romsey. The one intermediate station at Chandlers Ford closed to passengers in 1969, but the line remained open for freight. Passenger services and Chandlers Ford station were reinstated in 2003.

Above: A Class 33 is signalled for the Romsey line as the train approaches Alderbury Junction. The platforms were staff platforms only and not served by trains in the public timetable. Taken on an inexpensive snapshot camera in *c*1965, it is nevertheless a rarely photographed subject. (Courtesy of Dave Bevis)

Left: The morning Westbury to Eastleigh departmental about to pass under the Clarendon Road Bridge in Alderbury with Class 66 no. 66193 in charge on 20 April 2012. (SU 190 277)

The Wessex main line from Romsey to Redbridge forms part of the old 'sprat and winkle line' from Andover to Redbridge. The northern part from Andover to Kimbridge Junction (between Mottisfont and Dunbridge and Romsey) was closed under Beeching in September1964. This included a station at Mottisfont and the reason why Mottisfont was eventually added to the Dunbridge station name.

All the freight facilities at stations on the line were withdrawn long ago, but there remains a chalk quarry at East Grimstead, albeit now out of use. Trains ran from here to Quidhampton quarry, which itself closed in 2009.

Class 66 no. 66119 seen at East Grimstead with a short rake of Nacco chalk slurry tanks. These were known as silver bullets. A train of empties from Eastleigh came into Quidhampton Imerys quarry on each weekday morning and returned with loaded tanks before noon. Here the train is seen on its return journey on 2 November 2007. (SU 224 271)

Above: Class 66 no. 66007 passes the disused entrance to East Grimstead quarry with a Fawley to Bristol fuel tank service on 19 March 2007. (SU 225 271)

Right: East Grimstead disused quarry interior showing sidings on 1 March 2012. (Ref SU 227 271)

Dean station and signal box from an old postcard *c*1910.

Battle of Britain no. 34067 *Tangmere* approaches Dean station with a Victoria to Bristol enthusiasts'
excursion on 17 February 2007. Note the refuge siding, which has since been disconnected.
(SU 257 271)

The Wessex line from Southampton to Salisbury is a useful diversionary route when the
main line through Winchester is closed.

The principal passenger service on the line runs between Portsmouth and Cardiff and
includes Brighton and Malvern variations. Originally steam operated, it changed to Hymek
diesel hydraulic traction, followed by Class 33s then Class 158 diesel units to the present day.

Freight services include Somerset quarry stone traffic, Fawley fuel tanks, departmentals
between Westbury and Eastleigh and a few Freightliners from and to the docks.

A junction at Alderbury diverging south-west from the Bishopstoke and Salisbury route
(travelling from Salisbury) was opened in 1866. This is the route of the erstwhile Salisbury
& Dorset Junction Railway. This S&DJR should not be confused with the other S&DJR, the
Somerset and Dorset Joint Railway.

Class 60 no. 60072 *Cairn Toul* on the level crossing immediately west of Dean station platforms with a Whatley to Hamworthy stone boxes. (SU 257 271)

In Alderbury, there is a Junction Road, at the end of which are railway cottages, no doubt one of the reasons for the Alderbury Staff Platforms. The name of the road gives the game away, for this is where the S&DJR left the main line to Romsey, Bishopstoke (Eastleigh) and Southampton via Redbridge.

On 20 October 1860, it was proposed that a railway connecting Salisbury with Wimborne and Poole via Downton and Fordingbridge would be beneficial to Salisbury. The idea met with the approval of the meeting and an Act of Parliament received the Royal Assent in July 1861, which allowed for a junction at Alderbury and a single track line with station passing places to West Moors. At West Moors, it was planned to meet the Southampton and Dorchester Railway. Other schemes were put forward for extensions to the line but were aborted before any approvals were sought.

The first turf was removed from a field, reputedly with a silver spade, by Countess Nelson near Trafalgar House, north of Downton, on 3 February 1863. Trafalgar House was the home of the Earl and Countess Nelson. Following the death of the owner in 1813, Parliament acquired and gifted the estate to the heirs of Admiral Lord Nelson to commemorate the Battle of Trafalgar.

After the line was complete, it was inspected by the Board of Trade, which pinpointed a number of faults to be corrected before the railway could be opened for public use. It was approved to open on 20 December 1866.

On 31 May 1882, members of the S&DJR board met with the L&SWR directors to discuss amalgamation. This was approved and took effect from 20 August 1883.

This lovely cross-county railway line through the corners of Wiltshire, Hampshire and Dorset clearly did not pay its way. It closed to all traffic on 4 May 1964 and the track was lifted a year later. The only station on the Salisbury and Dorset Junction Railway in Wiltshire was at Downton, closing with the line in 1964. Today, the site has been redeveloped for housing and is aptly named The Sidings. The other stations affected by the closure were Breamore and Fordingbridge in Hampshire, and Daggons Road and Verwood in Dorset. Passenger trains were also withdrawn on the line through West Moors, where the S&DJR joined the S&DR, in May 1964.

Above left: A wonderful shot of the signalman and a lad at Alderbury Junction signal box, probably around 1910.

Above right: A Brownie 127 shot of Downton tunnel mouth in 1965. (Dave Bevis)

Left: Another shot taken on a Brownie 127 Bakelite camera of 75079 with a train on dismantling duties in 1965. The shot was taken near Standlynch not far from the site of the original first turf cutting in 1863. (Courtesy of Dave Bevis)

Downton station *c*1904. A postcard view towards Salisbury with a Bournemouth train about to enter the station.

L&SWR operated the route initially. After 1923, Southern Railway was in place, followed by the Southern Region after nationalisation in 1948. Locomotives were generally supplied by Salisbury shed.

The principal services were between Salisbury and Bournemouth West, with six trains a day each way. In 1952, longer distance cross-country trains were introduced, although few in number they connected the Dorset coast with South Wales.

Freight on the line was never particularly heavy, with watercress, strawberries (in season), grain and soft fruit predominating.

During its existence, there were two serious accidents on the line. The first on 3 June 1884 when the 16.33 Salisbury to Weymouth detached its carriages from the locomotive and derailed about 1¼ miles south of Downton. In total, 41 passengers were injured and four died, three of these drowning in a ditch after the carriage overturned. The cause was levelled on poor quality carriages travelling too fast for the line.

The second accident was on 2 November 1904 when a wagon, (possibly the brake van) from a Salisbury-bound freight broke away just south of Downton station. Despite a guard stopping the wagon, a Salisbury to Bournemouth train ploughed into it. Two people were injured.

Above: Another postcard view of Downton station taken just after the turn into the 20th century. A train from the Bournemouth direction is shortly to arrive. The station is crowded with many children.

Right: Downton station taken after closure in 1965. (Courtesy of Dave Bevis)

Bibliography

Bryan, T, *Brunel, The Great Engineer,* Ian Allan, 2004

Casserley, H C, *Wessex (Railway History),* David & Charles, 1975

Clew, R, *The Kennet and Avon Canal,* David & Charles, 1985

Corfield, M C, *A Guide to the Industrial Archaeology of Wiltshire,* Wiltshire County Council, 1978

Dalby, L J, *The Wilts and Berks Canal,* The Oakwood Press, 2000

Gagg, G, *The Observer's Book of Canals*, Claremont Books, 1996

Household, H, *The Thames and Severn Canal,* David & Charles, 1969

Lyons, E, *An Historical Survey of Great Western Engine Sheds 1947*, Oxford Publishing, 1972

Maggs, C G, *Rail Centres: Swindon,* Ian Allan, 1983

McKnight, H, *The Shell Book of Inland Waterways*, David & Charles, 1975

Mitchel, V, and Smith, K, *Branch Lines of West Wiltshire,* The Middleton Press, 2003

Mitchel, V, and Smith, K, *Fareham to Salisbury*, The Middleton Press, 1989

Mitchel, V, and Smith, K, *Salisbury to Westbury,* The Middleton Press, 1994

Mitchel, V, and Smith, K, *Westbury to Bath,* The Middleton Press, 1995

Morrison, B, *Great Western Steam at Swindon Works,* D. Bradford Barton, 1975

Roose, G, and Ballantyne, H, *Wiltshire,* Past & Present, 2002 edition

Sands, T B, *The Midland and South Western Junction Railway,* The Oakwood Press, 1990

Siviour, G, and Esau, M, *Waterloo – Exeter Heyday,* Ian Allan, 1990

Signals at the east end of Westbury station in 1979.